HONOR THY DAUGHTERS

A FATHER'S STORY OF A CHINA ADOPTION

Carlos Pineda

authorHOUSE®

AuthorHouse™
1663 Liberty Drive, Suite 200
Bloomington, IN 47403
www.authorhouse.com
Phone: 1-800-839-8640

First published by AuthorHouse 10/8/2008

ISBN: 978-1-4343-8830-8 (sc)
ISBN: 978-1-4343-8831-5 (hc)

Printed in the United States of America
Bloomington, Indiana

This book is printed on acid-free paper.

Dedicated to
Samantha Jun
and
in Loving Memory of

Beatriz Leal Pacheco

and William C. Stougaard

ACKNOWLEDGMENTS

Special thanks to all our friends and family who supported and diligently waited through the adoption process with us. Your love and understanding helped us through the tough waiting period. It was so worth the wait!

Thanks to Children's Hope International for walking us through the procedure in China, and for their help in getting this wonderful child. A special thanks for allowing us to represent them in our story.

Thanks to Wikipedia for information on the Forbidden City, Tiananmen Square, Teng Wang Pavilion, and the Great Wall of China. I am rather nonchalant about such matters.*

Special thanks to Melanie Walker for her valuable help in editing our story. Unfortunately, my vivid and creative imagination with words doesn't assist my syntax and sentence structure.

Thanks to the entire travel group who made the experience a wonderful memory. Special thanks to Geoff and Melody for all the special moments. I can't think of a better group to be a part of, and you will be dear to us forever!

I want to especially thank my loving wife, Lorraine, for her inspiration and support throughout the writing of this book. Her contributions and recollection of events and dates made it easier to reconstruct the trip. Her passion for life made the writing easy, and watching her joy with Samantha has been priceless.

FOREWORD

THE JOURNEY TO SAMANTHA WAS the most unique adventure I've ever been associated with. The people we met and the places we saw were inimitable. I stood on the steps of the Great Wall of China and was able to see the wall curve and wind through the mountains and valleys. It was humbling! I stood on the banks of the Pearl River and watched as the city of Guangzhou lighted up the sky at night. It was beautiful! I witnessed the street traffic, congested and busy with automobiles, motorcycles, scooters, pushcarts, bicycles hauling ox carts, and pedestrians scurrying past and around each other. Vehicles and pedestrians alike were all jockeying for position, all in the name of commerce—the product of a country with 1.8 billion people. I shall never forget these things!

I witnessed a city preparing to host the 2008 Olympic Games. The structural designs for some of the event buildings were phenomenal. The aquatic center and the track-and-field stadium would be architectural firsts—unique in their design and constructed like nothing else that exists today. The world is going to be in for a real delight. China is preparing for a gala event, and it is apparent that they do not plan on disappointing.

We were in China to get our daughter and take her home. This book chronicles our story through an ordinary and simple man's view. I wanted to enlighten everyone not so much with China's history, but with the journey of our adoption process.

Our travel group was an assortment of people from different parts of America and different walks of life. It made the fusion interesting. I thought most members of our group were generally considerate and cordial, but socializing was certainly not our main focus. I was intrigued by all the members of the group and tried to appreciate their individual stories of adoption, but for all of us, the daughters we would be meeting for the first time on this journey took precedence over anything else. Being part of this group made being Americans in a strange land a lot easier, and I wouldn't or couldn't think a better group to be a part of during this adventure. As much as we appreciated the camaraderie and friendship, to reference an old saying, "we all had bigger fish to fry."

It's hard to look at China through an unbiased lens. Being an American, it's hard to make a fair judgment on a place like China, where communist policies and old-world cultural attitudes rule. It's also a little hard to swallow that we are benefiting from the same rules and cultural biases that we scoff at. I look at Samantha and every day give thanks that I have been given the opportunity to make a better life for her. China may soon realize that the release of so many female children to adoption may be a big drawback for their country's future. I have learned quickly from the experience of raising two daughters previously and presently with Samantha how important it is to honor thy daughters. God does work in mysterious ways, because Samantha is the perfect child for us and has enriched our lives immensely.

I would like to tell everyone involved in the adoption process that in spite of the emotional roller coaster that it seems you're on, it does get better and you will forget it all when you finally hold your child. I didn't believe it when I was in line waiting, and I didn't think it would ever take away the hurt I experienced during our seemingly unending wait—I thought they were just words of sympathy, but it was true. To this day, I cannot remember what my life was like before the arrival of Samantha. The wait must be God's way of easing the transition, and recognizing how busy you're going to be for the next eighteen to twenty years.

THIS IS MY STORY.

CHAPTER ONE

I DON'T THINK I WILL ever find the words to describe how I felt the day I laid eyes on my daughter's picture for the first time.

Neither my family nor my friends would have ever believed that I would be in the final stages of an international adoption from China. It seemed out of character to those who thought they understood or knew me, but it had already been almost two years since we had begun the adoption process. There we were, knowing that we were close to meeting our child. We were waiting for the call and a photo of our daughter, joined by a long line of eager applicants who had endured the tedious procedure of completing the "dossier" and hoping for an opportunity to fulfill the dream of seeing their child's face for the very first time. We were ecstatic—finally one step closer to adopting our child. We were so very excited. We were so very naïve.

I am a Hispanic male and as such, am tied to many customs and beliefs: family values, cultural ties, and so forth. Adoption wasn't a common quest for our many families with double-digit sibling counts, and although it may be a stereotype, large families in our culture were not a myth but a reality. My grandmother and grandfather raised eleven children! It is easy to understand how adoption was far in the background for us. Although I was raised in the culture, my father was in the military, which offered us an opportunity to travel and see things most of my relatives were not privy to. This experience also allowed me to become my own person rather than a traditional, culturally-bound Hispanic male. The ability to think "outside the box" has been a blessing and a curse. Being able to do this has opened doors elsewhere for me in a variety of occupations that placed me in different cities and, unfortunately, at a distance from my family. I love my family and I miss them now more than ever, but I have created my own way and believe that I have benefited and prospered for doing so.

I grew up on the south side of San Antonio, Texas—the "circle," as it was called, and it was a rough place to grow up. I remember much of my teenage years with distaste and ill regard. The rough streets of our neighborhood with old, broken-down cars parked in backyards, gang signs painted on empty lots, and vacant homes and businesses depicted the poor conditions I called home. It was nobody's fault. That is just the hand I was dealt. I made the most of it and promised myself that I would not see myself in this place as an adult.

I have many childhood friends who still live in the neighborhood, struggling and seeking just to make a living, with no room or desire for advancement, content with just maintaining the status quo. I wanted more, and I knew that to get the life I wanted, I would have to leave. I realized this would mean leaving behind many of my family members, cousins, aunts, and uncles whom I truly admired.

I joined the army in 1974 and began to explore the world. When I returned briefly to San Antonio after my tour of duty, I found that nothing seemed to have changed in the four years I was gone. I was discouraged to see my old friends following in the footsteps of their parents and grandparents. Not only did they still live in the neighborhood, but some still lived with their parents. Other childhood friends had bought older homes in the same neighborhood as their parents. Family and cultural ties run deep.

I married a girl from my neighborhood when I returned from the service, and we quickly started a family. It was during that time that I found myself working just to survive like my old friends and realized I was headed down the same path as they were. I had promised myself more, but my young wife was content with the situation. These vastly different outlooks on life eventually led us to divorce. I wanted to seek new opportunities, whereas she only wanted to be close to home. These ties are profound and they can consume those involved. I knew that I would truly have to move on for good—a turning point I met with considerable sadness. Once I set the wheels in motion to leave that life behind, though, I never looked back. I moved north to Dallas within the year and never returned to live in San Antonio again.

My sole disappointment in the long wait for our new baby was that she wasn't able to meet my precious grandmother Beatriz Leal Pacheco. My life in San Antonio was my grandmother, my *abuelita,* and during my early teen years, I had been sent to live with her. When I went back to visit as an adult, her home was always my home base and everyone else would come to visit me there. She was a beautiful lady with a streak of mean, but living in that neighborhood, I understood! I really think she was the reason I lived long enough to get out of the "hood."

My grandfather passed away when I was young and my grandmother survived, like many, with his Social Security and Medicaid checks. She not only survived, but also took care of me. I was a handful, a typical, rebellious teenager who thought he knew everything. My grandmother was a special lady, and I made visiting her a priority as an adult, regardless of where I was living, especially during her last few years while she was in a nursing home. I wanted badly for her to meet and hold our new daughter, but my grandmother passed away on February 3, 2007, only a few months before we went to China. I still miss her terribly and cannot bear to remove her birthday from my calendar.

My current wife and I met thirteen years ago on a semi-blind date. She worked as a secretary for a law firm in Dallas and I was a manager of an oil-change shop in a nearby suburb. John was the manager who had trained me, and it was his wife who set up this so-called blind date. I had been single for quite some time and really hadn't enjoyed blind dates before, but John told me that his wife was setting me up with one of her coworkers regardless of how I felt about it. As luck would have it, John's wife worked at the same law firm as Lorraine. I say "so-called blind date" because a week before we were to meet at a barbecue at John's house, his wife brought Lorraine by the shop to "take a sneak peek." I liked her sense of humor and I definitely liked her. She was tall and blonde and a "smart ass," plus she was absolutely gorgeous. At that point, I was curious and interested to know if I had piqued her curiosity as well.

Lorraine and I realized almost immediately that we were soul mates. We became fast friends, and thirteen years later, she is still my best friend. We can talk for hours and we respect each other's opinions, even though we may not always agree. We came from different walks of life, but our hearts and souls were somehow destined to unite. Lorraine moved from North Carolina to Dallas on a whim. How fortunate for me since I lived in Dallas! Three months after she moved to Dallas, we met, and we married three months later in September 1995. We've been inseparable ever since.

Our different lifestyles and views have formed a strong foundation for our relationship. I live my life off the cuff, so to speak; there is none more prone to quick and reliable responses to business and family decisions than I am, whereas Lorraine is much more methodical and meticulous. Lorraine has a system for everything, and the contrast between her style and mine has worked very well for us. I am her Ricky and she is my Lucy. We have had thirteen wonderful years together, and I am counting on many more.

As we began the adoption process, I found that this journey would reveal things about myself I had not realized before. I would have new insights that would have never surfaced if not for the adoption experience.

CHAPTER TWO

WHEN LORRAINE AND I DECIDED a few years ago that we wanted to adopt a child, that's about all we knew. We had no idea where to start, what to do, how to do it, if we could afford it, or if we would even qualify. There were many questions, and we needed answers. As it turned out, our decision to adopt a child was the easiest part of the process. Lorraine and I had talked about adoption a couple of times early in our marriage, but just as idle conversation. It wasn't until 2005 that the possibility became a serious subject for us.

We looked at domestic adoption but found that the ins and outs—having to wait for our application to be picked out, being interviewed by the biological mother, hoping to get chosen, and so on—were things we were not at all prepared for. Then there was always the possibility the mother would change her mind. For Lorraine and me, this was not a good option.

When we starting looking at foreign adoption, the few options besides China included the programs in Guatemala, Colombia, the Republic of Kazakhstan, and Russia, and several of these countries required multiple visits. This would not be viable for Lorraine and me. Colombia's second visit required a twenty-eight-day stay. Kazakhstan and Russia had similar programs with multiple visits. Guatemala and China were the only one-visit adoption programs at the time and seemed much more practical for our means. We had heard that China had a very stable adoption program and had the impression the babies were well taken care of, but we put it on the back burner, because at first, we were leaning toward Guatemala.

We found an agency that did Guatemalan adoptions, and my wife sent in the application fee. Lorraine, or should I say the "investigator," decided to check out this agency and did some research. Nothing bad was said about the agency, but she kept seeing glowing comments about Children's Hope International and decided to contact them. They said that their Guatemala program was on hold and that they had a very strong program in China. There was that China thing again. After some discussion, we finally decided that China sounded like the right choice for us.

After some further research and talks with Children's Hope, we learned that the earliest age that China would allow their babies to be adopted was six months old. After the babies are abandoned, a search for the biological parents and family must be undertaken. Ads are run in the paper with the babies' pictures and information for a period of time. Also, the government believes that any mental or developmental disabilities that the babies might have been born with don't show up for at least six months.

Because of our age at the time we started the process—I was forty-eight and my wife was forty-two—we understood that we would probably get an older toddler. When we filled out our application with Children's Hope, there was a question on what age group we would be willing to accept, and we agreed that we would mark up to two years old. There was always the possibility that we would be matched with a child older than that, but we figured it was a starting point and decided we would be thrilled no matter what.

Lorraine quickly began the process of putting together our dossier. I let her take the lead and simply went where she told me to go and signed what she told me to sign. There weren't too many nights that I came home from work that I didn't find at least one document with a Post-it note filled with instructions for me.

Lorraine let me know that we had to go through a home study process and the dates we would be meeting with a social worker from a local agency. We had been living in Atlanta for about eight years, and Children's Hope did not have an office in our area at that time. They gave Lorraine the names of some local agencies that could perform the home study process.

At our first meeting, our social worker, Julia, asked us why we weren't going with Guatemala, because her agency had a good program and had lots of healthy baby boys ready to be adopted. I had two grown daughters from my previous marriage, so Lorraine and I thought raising a son together was definitely something to consider.

About a year before Lorraine and I had even thought about adopting, we were planning a trip to visit her sister, who was living in Belgium at the time. I hadn't traveled abroad in eighteen years so I needed to reapply for my passport. I sent the application only to be rejected, but I didn't understand why. I later learned from the passport office that the State of Texas was claiming I owed them $30,000 in back child support. During the Clinton administration, a law was passed that anyone who owed more than $5,000 in back child support would be denied a passport. I had been struggling with this issue for years, and after I married Lorraine, she took up the cause to see what could be done about getting those records cleared up.

I had fought for custody of my children when they were four and five years old. I was awarded temporary custody, but in the end, their mother and I shared joint custody. Through a glitch in the system, somehow the State of Texas had in their records that I owed them about $3,000. Well, I was young and struggling and couldn't pay that on top of my child support payments, so I hoped someone would realize their error and fix it. They did not. The state just began tacking on interest.

Several years after I married Lorraine, we went back to court and obtained custody of my children when they were eleven and twelve years old. Now my ex-wife was sending child support payments to me.

Lorraine with her usual optimism decided at one point that she was going to call the State of Texas and get things straightened out. After many calls and letters, she gave up in tears. The bureaucracy of the child support division in the State of Texas is the epitome of government at its worst. One lady even told my wife, "If your husband had made payments like he was supposed to, this wouldn't be happening." She was lucky Lorraine was four states away. We talked to a few attorneys and they wouldn't give us the time of day. Again, we gave up.

When we started the adoption process, it was with the certainty that Lorraine would be traveling by herself and that I would have to miss the opportunity of us being together to see our child for the first time. More than ever, I felt the sting of being a father in a one-sided system that usually favors mothers and has little regard for a "deadbeat dad." I am not a deadbeat dad! I was a victim of a poorly run system, and not being able to travel with Lorraine for our adoption kept me up at night.

So after we began the adoption process, we tried to find an attorney again. This time, we decided we would not give up until we found someone. It was difficult because most attorneys treated us like we were criminals and basically said we would need to offer a settlement and find a way to make a lump sum payment.

We kept trying and finally found someone who knew an attorney who might be willing to take the case. Feeling already beaten, we made the call to the last attorney on our list. We were a little put off by his mannerisms at first. He was a cocky attorney from New York who had relocated to San Antonio. However, he gave us hope, and we flung our hats into the ring. There was no overnight fix. Since we were living in Atlanta, we had to make several grueling trips to San Antonio that ended in disappointment.

We were almost ready to give up when our attorney came back to us with a new angle that was a little unorthodox and said, "Let's just give this a try." It was right before Christmas, and once more we traveled to San Antonio and sat through a hearing on pins and needles. We almost weren't going to be heard because the docket was so full. Our attorney had paced the halls with his cell phone in hand. Finally, after numerous calls, he found a judge who would hear our case in another courtroom. The opposing counsel was so sure of himself that he agreed not to have a court reporter take down the hearing. To everyone's surprise, the judge dismissed the entire amount and closed the case. We were even more surprised when the bailiff came over to congratulate us when the hearing was over. It's funny—you never know how people will perceive you, but he saw right through my ex-wife and her current husband to their greed. They could have set things straight with the state years before, but the prospect of a huge payday kept them from doing the right thing.

We were thrilled to win, and our attorney told us they couldn't appeal the case because it had not been recorded. We had to wait thirty days and then we would be home free.

Of course, we were practically devastated when our attorney called and said we had to go back to court yet again. They were trying to pull another rabbit out of a hat and wanted a new hearing based on "new" evidence. Another month went by with us on pins and needles before we had our day in court. The judge scowled when he saw my ex-wife and remembered who she was. My ex-wife turned out to be her own worst witness. The judge stuck with his prior decision, and as we were driving down the highway headed back home, we rolled down the windows and let out whoops of joy.

We will always be grateful to that attorney because he did what everyone said couldn't be done. In the end, we won and I reapplied for my passport. I remember the day it came in the mail. Lorraine and I did a dance of joy. The eighteen months of traveling back and forth from Georgia to Texas had been hard and had taken its toll on us mentally, physically, and financially. The process had set us back $6,000 in travel expenses. It was worth every cent, though, because Lorraine and I had other important places to go.

Chapter Three

Surely, with the way things worked out with the child support situation, meeting and marrying my wife ... you know I truly do believe in fate and destiny and all that. After going through this process, my belief in destiny has only become stronger. Let me explain a little about the dossier process. Besides having to get all kinds of paperwork pulled together, we had to go through Homeland Security and get approval to bring home an orphan from China. Lorraine had sent that application in several weeks before our first home study meeting. She had sent it by certified mail but had yet to receive the green card saying that the immigration office had received our application.

After our meeting with Julia, we were convinced that Guatemala was the way to go, but now we would have to redo our application with Homeland Security to get approval to bring home a baby from Guatemala. If you've ever had to work with any immigration or government office at all, you know that what my wife was able to do was just amazing. First, she put a stop payment on the check, and then she called the immigration office. She actually got someone on the phone that searched for and found our application and agreed to send it back to us. Apparently, our application was just sitting on someone's desk and they hadn't even sent the return receipt card back. Just to be on the safe side, Lorraine suggested we wait until we got this application back before we submitted the new one for Guatemala. This interruption gave us a few days to think.

In those few days, my resolve to adopt from Guatemala wavered. I couldn't stop thinking about a little girl from China. I kept this to myself and decided to keep reviewing the options since we had a few days' reprieve. The more I thought about it, the more I wrestled with our decision to change to the Guatemala program. I couldn't get that little girl out of my head, but I didn't know how to tell my wife because she seemed so excited by the change we had made. Then, just as she was sitting down to fill out the new application, she turned to me and said, "I'm not sure about this; I can't get the little Chinese girl out of my head." I was so relieved that we were back on the same page.

It had to be fate, because when we sent our application back to Homeland Security to bring home a Chinese baby, we got our return receipt within two days, and we got our approval about a month before we were told to expect it. In other words, we pulled our application from someone's desk who was very slow and switched it to a person who knocked it right out.

So when people ask us, Why China? Our answer is simple: Because that's where our daughter was.

CHAPTER FOUR

AFTER THAT, THE PROCESSING OF our dossier went out without incident. Well, it did as far as I know, anyway. Lorraine was diligent and committed to the dossier process, and I must say I was impressed with how quickly she completed the task. This may have been the easiest time in the whole process for us. Even though there was much to do, we kept busy, and we felt like we had control over how the process was going and how long it was taking. The day came to send the dossier to our agency, and we got a card in the mail saying it had been sent to China.

Our dossier was then sent to the review room of the China Center of Adoption Affairs (CCAA). The first step for all dossiers is the review room, where the CCAA makes sure that everything is in order and they have all the information they need. When the review is finished, the dossier is "logged in." For us, this process took about thirty days.

We then got a phone call and a card in the mail from Children's Hope saying our dossier had been logged in with the CCAA and that our magical log-in date (or LID as we would come to call it) was October 27, 2005. This date will be engraved in our minds and hearts forever. The LID date is very important because from the review room, dossiers are sent to the matching room. From there, the wait begins for the dossiers to be matched with "paper-ready" babies. Once a month, the CCAA matches the paper-ready babies with the dossiers based on the next LIDs in line. At that time, the CCAA was matching more than a month's worth of LIDs each month. We were told our wait would be about eight months from the date of our LID, so we expected to travel in the summer of 2006.

Through some research on the Internet, we learned of a lady who was also adopting from China, and who many said had reliable sources of information not available to the ordinary layman. We began following her Web page and learned the wait would indeed increase to eighteen months and possibly longer. We followed her Web site, studying about the adoption process and learning where to find other resources and facts. The dependency on her information kept thousands of waiting families in a feeding frenzy, and the CCAA eventually heard about her involvement. As a result, she had to set ground rules, and it became more and more difficult to receive information in advance. Her following was enormous, and for good reason. Her accuracy in predicting cut-off dates for LIDs each month was amazing. When we started following along, we promised ourselves that we would not let it consume us, but we found ourselves addicted. We did not want to believe what we were reading, but soon had to accept the awful truth.

The news about the increasing wait time was discouraging, and we grew tired of having to explain the delay to everyone, all the time, so we just stopped talking about the whole thing. We told ourselves it would be better if we shifted gears and concentrated on other things that needed to be done, like finishing the nursery. The nursery was a fun project for us, especially for me. I wanted to have a Dr. Seuss theme and began searching the Internet for pictures, paintings, and wall decorations. The sites were limited because of copyright issues, and the items for sale were rather expensive. We were on a tight budget, especially since we knew the cost of the upcoming trip to China, so I improvised. My mother-in-law had a light scope projector that would enlarge a picture and illuminate it on the wall. This made it easy to trace, but that's where the easy part ended. I've always been good at doodling and drawing caricatures, but I had never tried my hand at painting. After tracing the images on the wall, I outlined them with a brush in black paint. I filled them in with color and took Advil for the cramps in my fingers and the pain in my back from stooping over for the next three months as I finished Samantha's nursery. Although I succeeded in completing the nursery walls with the Dr. Seuss theme, I failed at keeping the adoption in the background. We discussed it less than we used to, but it was always there.

In the summer of 2006, almost a year after we had started the adoption process, we found out that Lorraine's brother, James, was getting married in September. Someone suggested that I be the DJ. I have always been involved in music, whether it was as a youth playing in local cover bands or as an adult handling sound for a country-and-western band. I was intrigued, but I needed equipment.

Lorraine is still perplexed about how I persuaded her to buy $3,000 worth of sound and DJ equipment. I'm slick, but not $3,000 worth of slick, if you know what I mean. It wasn't as simple as it sounds, talking Lorraine into an investment this large, even if it was initially for her brother's wedding.

We were tired of the stress and the wait and answering questions like, "When are you going to China?" or "Are you still doing the adoption thing?" Lorraine and I needed a distraction, and that's when the idea hit. If we did this for James's wedding, could we do this on a regular basis and form a business opportunity out of the project? That's when C & L Music Company was formed, and it definitely helped take our minds off the waiting process. As of this writing, it's been a three-year project, and we are still in business.

Time marched slowly on. February, March, and April 2007 were rough months because the CCAA matching room was getting very close to our LID. By the end of February, the CCAA had matched through October 13th, and we just knew we were next. You couldn't possibly understand how tired I grew of hearing the line, "Something has happened that has never happened before." It wore at my very core. That statement seemed to be the catchphrase for the months of March and April. March came and the anticipation was growing. The CCAA had matched October 14th through the 24th—we had just three days to go—but it was April that turned out to be the straw that broke the camel's back. The CCAA matched only two days—October 25th and 26th. They had missed us by just one day! Lorraine broke down. I felt like screaming, but I needed to hold it together for Lorraine. I knew the wait had taken its toll on her when I heard her tell her mother, "I just can't put a positive spin on this; I'm losing hope that I'll ever see my daughter." I had never in my life felt this kind of emotion. I cried.

I don't think I'd cried like that since I'd seen *Brian's Song*, the Brian Piccolo story. (I may have been eight years old.) This 1971 movie was an autobiographical account about a friendship between football player Brian Piccolo and Hall of Fame running back Gale Sayers that was cut short when Piccolo developed cancer and died. I was that broken hearted.

CHAPTER FIVE

IT HAD BEEN SIXTEEN MONTHS, and Lorraine and I had decided to start the final countdown to our referral, which means that a dossier has been matched with a baby. *Referral* was the magic word. There were other terms or jargon, some of which drove us crazy, terms like *paper pregnant* and *Gotcha Day* that seemed silly and trite. Lorraine and I had tried to put the adoption in the background of our lives so it would not consume us.

After reading the blogs and Web sites designated for families in the waiting period of the adoption process, saying that many adoptive parents were consumed would be an understatement. Lorraine and I were determined not to let this happen to us. We are very realistic. We know there are things we have no control over. This was one of those things. We understood that no one "owed" us a baby and that it had nothing to do with "fairness." I did feel bad for these families because I knew what they were feeling. I knew how easy it was to fall into regret and hopelessness. We weren't going down that road! There was probably an underlying reason that Lorraine and I had such disdain toward some of the terms and phrases used by other waiting families. It may have been connected to the whining and unjustified venting that travel through some of the adoption blogs, too. I only know how we felt, and although we tried to relate to how others might feel, we thought it was somewhat exaggerated, and that alone made it hard to sympathize. Because Lorraine and I are realists, we know "it is what it is." It's a sinful waste of time to worry about things that you have no control over.

May had finally rolled around. I couldn't blame Lorraine for not wanting to get her hopes up, but I was a believer this time. There was no way we could not be in; we were next! I had felt the sting of being left out two months in a row, and no longer would I be a victim. Today was the day! I jumped out of bed at 5:30 A.M. and got on the computer to check our e-mail. There was a quote from our agency saying that the CCAA had matched dossiers with LIDs through October 30, 2005. I quickly printed off the e-mail and ran back to the bedroom to show my wife. She was awake but still blinked a few times as she read the e-mail, almost afraid to believe it was true, that the day was finally here. We held each other and cried. The waiting was nearing its end, and we knew we would see the bubbly little face of our new daughter soon. We were beside ourselves. No one word could express what we were feeling.

Lorraine called me at work later that day and said our agency representative had just called her from the Children's Hope Nashville office and given us the preliminary information on our daughter. Her name was Wang, Qiu Fu and she was six-months-old. And even more coincidental, her birthday was October 27, 2006. One year to the day from our original LID date. How's that for destiny? It suddenly explained the long wait. It had taken this long because we had to wait for our daughter to be born and become paper ready.

We were thrilled but also a little shocked that we had gotten such a young baby. Like I said earlier, because of our age, we expected an older child, so we were even more excited at the prospect of being able to start getting to know her at such a young age.

The agency e-mailed us a small black-and-white photo of our daughter that afternoon. Lorraine and I were on the phone with each other waiting for that e-mail. We wanted to see it together in the only way we could since we were both at work. I opened the e-mail attachment and was absolutely speechless for several minutes. I felt the warm tears rolling down my face as I gazed at the photograph of a child I had been impatiently, conscientiously, and restlessly waiting to see for nearly two years. She had chubby cheeks, and her hair stood straight up on her head like a little Mohawk. Lorraine and I couldn't hold back the tears of joy that overtook us in that moment. We were in love!

We forgot we were at work, and my coworkers were all staring at me, puzzled at my reaction since I am not known as a warm and fuzzy kind of person, but I couldn't help myself. I don't think I really wanted to.

The agency had promised to send the document package overnight with the original color pictures of Samantha from the orphanage along with some of the documents that required our signatures that same day. However, once again, something happened that had never happened before, and by accident, the documents were not sent out. It was rumored that someone lost their job over this, but it meant that we would not get our package until the next day. We found ourselves waiting again!

Referral Announcement

CHAPTER SIX

I MENTIONED EARLIER THAT SOME of the jargon or phrases used tried our patience. *Paper pregnant* was one that floated around the blogs and Web sites. I'm not trying to anger or belittle anyone, but I'd like to share our feelings on the subject, and it is after all just an opinion. I want to explain why this term rubbed us the wrong way. Lorraine and I had had all the medical tests and counseling that couples who want to have a family usually have, and we just seemed to fall short. A few days before Lorraine went in for an exploratory surgery, we had sat and talked about the possibility of trying to adopt a child. Sadly, the final diagnosis came back that Lorraine would probably never become pregnant. This was after the doctor had performed the surgery and realized that Lorraine's endometriosis was so severe that pregnancy was more or less impossible.

This, of course, broke her heart, but again, we are very realistic people who believe that when one door closes, another door usually opens. It definitely helped that we had already decided that we would look into adoption. It didn't take us long to rebound from the medical conclusion and begin seeking information about the adoption process. Here's the bottom line: Just because you can't get pregnant and you can't have your own "biological children," that doesn't lessen your ability to be parents. In a way I think your willingness to move past that and find other resources to accomplish what you seek puts you ahead of a lot of people. The ability to think "outside the box" opens up many other doors. Not being able to get pregnant is not a failure; it is a challenge for those who really want to raise a child, and people should in no way feel "less than" or slighted because they cannot get pregnant. And believe me, the love and connection you feel for an adopted child is just as deep and fulfilling as the feelings for a biological child. It can really be one of the most special things you will feel in your life—a cosmic connection, if you will. Some people who have children are sadly not capable of parenthood, so be proud, be diligent, and let's come up with a new term for the dossier, something like *forever file*. We all know it felt like it took forever to put that large file together.

CHAPTER SEVEN

OUR FAMILY MEMBERS BEGAN TO receive the news that Lorraine and I were finally looking at a photo of our daughter, and with the lightning-fast delivery of e-mail, they, too, were able to gaze at our daughter's pretty face. The matching room of the CCAA truly does work magic. I had read through the many blogs and rumor Web sites that they match babies to parents in different ways. It would seem logical that the CCAA would match first by the parents' request—the preferred age of a child, a special medical-needs child, or a non-special needs child—and the prospective parents' ages also played a role in the process. The rumor was that the CCAA also tried to physically match the child with the appearance and features of the adopting father.

This was what we believed happened to Lorraine and me, because Wang, Qiu Fu had a scary resemblance to me. I was amazed at how much she looked like me. I have been told I look a little like I could be from the Philippines. Our family was also amazed at the resemblance. Everyone in our family who endured the wait, followed us through the paperwork process, and rode the emotional roller coaster as it tested our wills over and over was excited beyond words. It was a glorious time for everyone!

In hindsight, I remember that most of the daughters adopted by the families in our travel group bore a strong resemblance to the fathers, and in some cases, the mothers. Go figure!

We had decided that our daughter's christening name would be Samantha Jun Pineda, although we figured we would leave her middle name open in case we could incorporate her Chinese name. We used *Jun* because in the Chinese language, it translates to "honesty." We also thought it had a nice ring to it. We started marking her territory by stenciling, embroidering, and painting her name everywhere in her nursery. Going overboard doesn't begin to describe our enthusiasm, but we didn't care. We wanted everyone to see, hear, and know her name, and we wanted to shout it from the highest mountaintop.

When we saw that all the children in our group were named "Wang Qiu" something, we realized this wasn't the name given to her by her biological family but by the institution, kind of like a number or how in America, we name hurricanes. So in the end, we stuck with the name that we had lovingly labored over.

I have to take a moment to recognize all the support we received from our friends and family during the whole process. Our family and closest friends truly did share our enthusiasm, and when we got our referral, they kicked it up a notch. Friends and coworkers threw baby showers, and we received many gifts in the mail. It wasn't just the generosity that touched us so much but the genuine enthusiasm we felt from everyone that was just overwhelming.

Many times during that long wait for our referral, it was easy to feel very alone. Our friends and family let us know definitively that they were right there with us, and for that, I am forever grateful.

Lorraine and I spent the next two months after our referral planning and preparing for our trip to China. As I began to add up the cost, I felt my stress and anxiety level climbing to scary heights. How were we ever going to afford this? Lorraine has been my wife for thirteen years and has been my closest friend and adviser, too. It seemed she had already figured that part of the equation. Lorraine has been the brain trust of our marriage, and she is the reason we have kept our heads above water and actually had a small nest egg to boot.

We started a Web site for our new daughter and documented our visit to China. I've included some of my journal entries in this book.

Journal entry pre-trip

Actual Itinerary for China

Date: 06/12/2007

Date Itinerary Hotel

Fri, June 22—Arrive in Beijing Radisson SAS

Sat, June 23—Sightseeing in BJ: Tiananmen Square & Forbidden City, the Great Wall (Juyongguan). Lunch is included; Orientation

Sun, June 24—Flight to Nanchang: MU5174(10:50a–13:05p) Meet child in the afternoon Gloria Plaza Hotel

Mon, June 25—Do the registration and notary

Tue, June 26—Free day

Wed, June 27—Sightseeing: TengWeng Pavilion in the morning

Thur, June 28—Sightseeing: Countryside

Fri, June 29—Get the passport and all paperwork back, do paperwork for the ACS, flight to Guangzhou

MU5231(17:10p–18:35p) White Swan Hotel

Sat, June 30—Medical examination for children

Sun, July 1—Free day

Mon, July 2—Appt at ACS, Farewell Dinner

Tues, July 3—Go to ACS to take oath and get the visa in the afternoon around 6 P.M.

Wed, July 4—Departure to U.S.

I remember the packing fiasco with humor, but I really thought it was a test of our marriage. I am a stickler for detail, and I had read a lot of literature on what they recommended to pack for the trip, both for Lorraine and me and the baby. I looked up the allowable weight restrictions for both domestic and international flights and thought we should follow the rules, whereas Lorraine had little regard for rules and regulations. If Lorraine thought she needed it, by God, she was packing it. This was a source for many disagreements and a lot of repacking. In the end I really don't know who won—I may have, but the compromise kept our marriage intact.

As we prepared to travel to China, Lorraine and I had our list of all the things we needed to take with us. On our list were gifts for the orphanage director, the notary, and various other department heads along with the required fees for various departments. The list was long and the cost was hefty, but I found the gift exchange to be interesting. We were instructed to bring the fee monies in cash— brand new, unwrinkled, unsoiled crisp bills in various denominations. I later discovered that an international adoption is the only way a bank will allow you to get that amount of money in new bills. I was worried because I would have to carry that amount of money with me throughout the whole trip! I wanted a money belt and a six foot, seven inch bodyguard!

The day before we were scheduled to fly out, Pam and Darlene, our good friends from Raleigh, North Carolina, drove into town. They had volunteered to house-sit and take care of our two dogs while Lorraine and I were in China. They joined us for a good-bye dinner along with several of our local friends at an Irish pub in Marietta named Johnny McCracken's. Renee, Jennifer, and Suzy met us there, and we had a great time visiting and having dinner. I must say I welcomed the interruption from the stress of our packing and going through our final checklist. It was also nice to know how much our friends truly cared and supported us throughout the process. We thanked them and asked to be remembered in their prayers as we bid our good-byes, because the following day was the beginning of our journey to Samantha.

Chapter Eight

WE LEFT HARTSFIELD–JACKSON INTERNATIONAL AIRPORT at 8:30 A.M. on June 22, 2007, with our first stop in Minneapolis. Pam and Darlene drove us to the airport. As we hugged each other good-bye, Darlene said, "Wow, when we pick you up, there will be three of you."

We checked our baggage and headed for the long security lines in Hartsfield, hoping it wouldn't take forever. Although we had been warned to expect a four-hour delay, we were through security in about two hours. We were still pretty fresh and alert when we arrived in Minneapolis and we had a small layover, so we went to the closest watering hole at the airport, Wolfgang Puck, got a snack, and downed a few cold ones. The watering hole had a rather large waitress with blonde pigtails. She had sort of a Viking look and talked with the area accent. All I remember hearing was "aei and yaw." We departed from Minneapolis at 1:45 P.M. headed for Tokyo. With an eleven-hour flight ahead of us, and rattled nerves, I took the time to reflect on the previous twenty-two months of a grueling waiting period, if anything just to take my mind off such a long flight. I couldn't believe we were now just days away from meeting our daughter. Once we arrived in Tokyo at Narita International, we still had one more leg of the trip to complete before landing in Beijing.

During the long flight from Minneapolis, Lorraine sat next to a young Korean woman who was going home because of her ill father.

She had left her two children back home in the States and was worried about them and her ailing father. She and Lorraine shared their life stories. It was heartbreaking to know how sad and concerned she was for her family, whereas all the while Lorraine and I were champing at the bit with joy. I took a few moments and said a silent prayer for her and her family. When we arrived in Tokyo, she boarded a different bus to a different terminal and just like that was gone. I hope all went well.

Our arrival in Tokyo at Narita International was unique for me since I can't remember the last time—could have been twenty years or more—that I departed a plane on a rolling staircase. We were out in the open landing strip very much like the president descending the stairs off Air Force One. I know it's a little exaggerated, but that's what crossed my mind!

It was in Tokyo that we learned that there had been another family from Children's Hope with us on the flight from Minneapolis to Tokyo. They were the first traveling companions we encountered from a group of fifteen families Children's Hope was sending to China to bring home their adopted daughters. They were from the St. Louis area, and I couldn't help but be grateful that we now had a common bond with someone else. It was a stressful time, and knowing we weren't alone helped out tremendously. We were to find out later that there were many more families on that last flight from Tokyo. Some were from different countries such as Spain, France, and other parts of Europe, all going to the People's Republic of China for the same reason. It was absolutely fascinating!

Narita International was as spectacular and as modern an airport as any I've ever seen. I had seen photographs of the airport while searching the Internet for information about Narita, but it was even more impressive live and in color. We waited for about an hour before our last connecting flight that would put us in China. I walked about the airport looking for a smoking room. I knew some airports didn't accommodate smokers, but I was optimistic from what I'd read about how the majority of the Asian population enjoyed and didn't ostracize smoking. I found the smoking room, and it was as disgusting as any airport smoking room I've been in. It made me wonder what I saw in this filthy habit. The room had no seats, just a funny-looking contraption with about four cigarette lighters; they looked like your ordinary car cigarette lighter, but stuck out of a trash can. While I grabbed a smoke, Lorraine went to McDonald's for some coffee with our newfound friends. When she got back, she relayed all that she had learned from them. She learned about the potty-training process in the orphanages, which is pretty rough, I can tell you. She also learned that most of the babies and toddlers wear split pants instead of diapers.

Hearing the announcement of other flights arriving and departing in the Japanese dialect made us realize that we were definitely out of our element, and it felt strange. Lorraine and I sat quietly, drinking our coffee and ruminating over our last days as just a couple. We were about to become a family. It was time to board our flight to China. We were silent. We were nervous. We were scared!

CHAPTER NINE

WE ARRIVED IN BEIJING AROUND 9:45 P.M. and were enthusiastically met at the airport by the Children's Hope agency representatives Elaine and Gloria, who gracefully and professionally led us through the entire process and turned out to be spectacular tour guides. Elaine was the experienced veteran of the two and was actually very entertaining. Elaine was accompanied by Gloria, a very young and wide-eyed trainee of sorts, who I think actually received more from this experience than she had bargained for. Elaine and Gloria had someone collect the group's luggage, and we were off to the Beijing Radisson Hotel. The shuttle ride was interesting, and we eagerly took in our first views of Beijing. Elaine quickly began to give us a history lesson on the toll bridge road we needed to take to get to Beijing. The story went that the toll charge was so expensive that several hurricanes had veered off their course to avoid paying the toll. There would be many such stories like this one in the next fourteen days.

Elaine was probably twenty-five or twenty-six years old. I assumed Gloria to be a few years younger, barely twenty-one, but it was Elaine who kept your attention. Elaine's English was shaky at times, but it was her heavy accent that made everything she said hysterically funny. Even if the subject wasn't supposed to be funny, there was always a touch of humor in the delivery. This made all our trips together much more interesting for me; I'm not sure about the rest of the group. I think they sometimes struggled to understand Elaine's version of English. I was used to choppy English, so I had no problems understanding Elaine; go figure. Gloria was very quiet and seemed to play the "sidekick" role very well. It was like Vanna White's role on *Wheel of Fortune*, turning letters while Pat Sajak did all the talking. Elaine did all the talking, and she was not shy.

We pulled into the Radisson Beijing Hotel around 11 P.M. and quickly checked in with the desk clerk, who was extremely polite and pleasant. We went to our room to wait for the luggage, which was ten minutes behind us. Everyone we had encountered so far was very professional and exceptionally polite. I wondered if this was the norm or if it was because the City of Beijing was in the process of preparing for the 2008 summer Olympic Games. I had seen a news special on the History Channel about some of the Olympic structures and the difficulties construction workers were going to have with assembling some of these groundbreaking designs. China was set to be center stage for the world, and the Chinese government was pulling out all the stops in the development of some of the most remarkable architectural masterpieces created solely for the 2008 games. The Bird's Nest was a structure created with steel beams crisscrossing and going in all directions, hence its name. The aquatic center was going to be a new revelation as architectural designs go. This was probably one of the most spectacular buildings to ever be designed, and should they complete it in time for the 2008 Olympics, it will be a beautiful sight. China was preparing for the world! The hospitality was in full bloom as they prepared to expose their country to the world's analytical eyes, and unfortunately China's controversial adoption process, human rights issues, and the one-child rule were in full view to be scrutinized!

We unpacked a little in our hotel room and tried to settle in, but would have a very restless night ahead of us.

Beijing is like a ghost town at 4 A.M. I hadn't adjusted to the time change and had trouble sleeping, so I rose early to take a stroll around the hotel. I thought at first that I might have overslept, but sunrise comes early in China. I witnessed early morning workers on bikes, and motorbikes hauling carts of produce ready for sale at the local marketplace. By 5:30 A.M., the city was coming alive. Shopkeepers began opening their garage-like doors for business, and young men had gathered in a courtyard across the street to play basketball. Basketball is a very popular sport in China, and with Chinese nationals like Yao Ming being drafted by the American NBA, it is gaining in popularity. I was starting to feel alive and I began to appreciate several things. I was in China and it was beginning to register in my mind that this was going to be a life-changing event. Lorraine and I would never be the same! This was the trip of all trips, the grandest vacation we would ever take, and it was to have the happiest ending of any story we've been a part of. We were going to have to be patient and wait for one more day before we would get to meet our daughter, who was waiting in the province of Jiangxi.

CHAPTER TEN

Children's Hope had prepared us for the trip by planning the itinerary and giving us a list of all the families that would be traveling with us. Some of the families had opted to fly into Hong Kong instead of Beijing and would meet up with us in Nanchang. Most of our children were from the Social Welfare Institute of Yujiang in the province of Jiangxi, People's Republic of China, and some from smaller orphanages. The children are all girls and ranged from eight to twelve months in age. We had one family who was adopting an older, special-needs child from a different province and they would be meeting up with our group in Guangzhou, which was our last stop. It seemed far away at that point.

Journal entry one

We've Arrived!

Date: 06/22/2007

We got in at 11 last night. The travel was grueling and uneventful. We met a few families last night and will meet the rest when we go to Nanchang. Our Children's Hope representatives met us at the airport and Elaine is adorable. She told us a lot of funny stories and she will be with us for our whole trip. We're staying at the Radisson here in Beijing and it's very nice. The staff is very helpful and even opened the computer center early for us.

Today, we're leaving at 8:30 A.M. for the Great Wall, Tiananmen Square, and the Forbidden City. Tomorrow, it's off to Nanchang to meet our daughter.

The itinerary had us meeting in the lobby Saturday morning at 8 A.M., June 23, 2007, where we would start our first journey together as a group. I started to encounter some of the other family members from Children's Hope in the lobby of the Beijing Radisson around 6 A.M. We made our introductions and some small talk, but I was eager to see if the business center was open. The business center was still closed, and I really wanted to get in there so I could update our Web site. I asked the front desk for the business center's hours. It may have been just great service or that the staff was practicing for the 2008 Olympic Games performance, but they opened the business center for me at 6:10 A.M., which impressed me since the normal opening time was 8 A.M. It wasn't the only time in the next few days that the service from this Beijing staff would impress me. If this was any indication of the service they will provide for the 2008 games, the world is in for a pleasant surprise.

The easiest way for us to communicate with our family back home proved to be our Web site. It was almost impossible to connect with the overseas operator using the hotel telephone service in Beijing. We had read in the blogs about several companies that would provide phones with international service for groups traveling in China. One of these companies provided the Panda Phone. How ironic! Lorraine and I opted for an international calling card and it worked only 50 percent of the time. When we were able to connect with someone back home, it was too cool. It might be better for those who travel to China in the future to invest in something like the Panda phone.

Tiananmen Square (Beijing)

CHAPTER ELEVEN

ELAINE AND GLORIA CAME IN carrying Children's Hope flags, was accompanied by a very short, thin, Chinese lady in a schoolgirl-ish kind of outfit. She had large, black, round glasses and looked like Edna Mode, otherwise known as "E" from *The Incredibles*, the animated movie by Pixar. Eve was the name she gave us. She was very knowledgeable about China's history, which was why she was there. Lorraine had made me watch the movie *The Last Emperor* before leaving for China because there was a possibility we would be touring the Forbidden City. I would later remember calling it the "Forever City" because the tour was so long.

We started out the morning with a stop at Tiananmen Square. *It was built in 1417 during the Ming dynasty. In 1699 during the early Qing dynasty, Tiananmen Square was renovated. It seemed like the proper curriculum for an American tourist. The Forbidden City was next on our busy schedule. The Forbidden City was built back in the early 1400s. It was established as a World Heritage Site in 1987 by the United Nations Educational, Scientific and Cultural Organization (UNESCO) as the "Imperial Palace of the Ming and Qing Dynasties" because of its importance in the development of Chinese architecture and culture. The history was interesting, but in a nutshell, the idea of seeing and touching structures that were built six or seven centuries ago is remarkable, and that alone intrigued me. The only turnoff to the tour was a spot of commercialism built smack in the middle of the Forbidden City in the form of a Starbucks coffee store.

The preparation for the 2008 Olympic Games was very evident in the Forbidden City, because many of the buildings were being refurbished and the landscape was being attended to. As the Chinese would say, "It's being made fresh." The most unusual sight was seeing two elderly ladies weeding the vast brick courtyard. It was fascinating, but it looked like a lot of work for two women. The fine attention to detail that China is taking for the presentation of their country will certainly impress the world during the Olympic Games.

As we walked back to the bus, we were immediately gang-rushed by aggressive vendors in the square selling kites and bottled water. We'd been warned that the bottled water might be recycled bottles filled with boiled water, and then frozen. It was probably safe to drink, but we thought it best not to take chances. They weren't like vendors here in America; those vendors were very antagonistic, and it was almost a scary assault, yet I still found the whole thing amusing.

We all loaded back on the tour bus and went to eat lunch at a restaurant in Beijing's downtown area famous for its Peking duck. It was a pleasant surprise since my first experience with duck had not gone smoothly. The gamey taste had not set well with my spoiled palate. This was different, and I enjoyed the meal tremendously.

We sat with a family from Arkansas who had brought along their two young sons. It was a good meal, and we enjoyed the company during dinner. Every restaurant that we visited in Beijing sported the same type of setting. There was a lazy Susan—at least that was how Lorraine referred to it—a Plexiglas sphere that carousels around the table allowing everyone access to each item of food served. There were blue-colored tofu balls and twenty varieties of noodles along with a long-neck, headless duck. Despite the appearance, most everything was tasty.

There was a small bowl of soup-like substance, and I remember daring the boys to try it. I eventually went first and remarked how it tasted a bit like dish soap. I chuckle now, because I believe it was a fingerbowl to rinse your fingers in while eating the duck. The boys probably thought we were crazy for willingly taste-testing all the items, but we had fun. There were several families who had brought along their children, and I was impressed by their excellent behavior during this grueling, fast-paced trip.

After our meal, we walked across the street to the Children's Hope Beijing office headquarters for an orientation and a short film. The Children's Hope representatives talked about what was in store for us as we traveled into the Chinese countryside to get our children. They discussed the various customs and traditions of the people we would meet in these rural districts. They showed us a film commemorating other families' unions with their daughters. There wasn't anyone in the room who withstood the emotional heartstring plucking of this short film. I had to leave and get some air. I found myself easily affected in these situations, which surprised me, because I've never been that emotional. This would be the last time I felt warm and fuzzy about the program; I would soon become very cynical. We gathered ourselves as a group and loaded into the bus for our final tour of the day—the Great Wall of China.

Eve, or "E," as I referred to her, did her job and completely inundated us with all the facts and history of each site we visited. It was funny because she knew we were focusing our attention elsewhere, but it did not impede her from telling us anyway. On the bus ride to the Great Wall, she even said, "I know you will probably not listen or go to sleep, but that's okay, I keep talking anyway." I regret in a way that I didn't pay closer attention to her, since in one day I would be holding a Chinese native. There may come a time when that information needs to be passed to our Chinese daughter. Culture is important, but at that moment, I seemed to be clueless!

One family member thought Eve was a communist infiltrator . . . contracted by Children's Hope but Children's Hope had no idea she was a spy. He was only half joking. Mao Tse Tung was definitely "great" to her. She was definitely an admirer of Mao. Eve reminded us over and over of how great he was and of his struggles, but then with a huge grin, she told us that in the end "we won."

I have found that most Americans—not all, but a large majority of them—hold certain things to be true: there is a leaning tower somewhere in Italy, there are some kind of ruins in Rome, there is a large waterfall that borders Canada and the United States, and China has a man-made wall that is three thousand miles long and they say you can see it from outer space. We, for the most part, are very blasé about those things!

If you have ever wondered what it would be like to stand atop a mega structure that was under construction around the seventh century B.C., it is awe-inspiring to think of its construction and the battles that took place on that wall. The mountainside was decorated with the wall as it snaked and wound through and around valleys and cliffs; it was a very humbling experience. *The wall was built to withstand the attacks of small arms such as swords and spears, and was made mostly by compacted soil and gravel between plank frames. Transporting the resources needed to build the wall was very complex, so the builders tried to use the resources of the mountain itself such as stones, gravel, and dirt. The steps were of various shapes and measurements, and climbing them was very dangerous. It was even more dangerous coming down. Lorraine and I started at the bottom of the North Pass of Juyongguan, known as Badaling. This section of the wall was used to defend China's capital city of Beijing. We climbed up the uneven steps toward the top of the two towers. I made it to the first tower and realized that I valued breathing and life, so I took a rest while Lorraine continued on to the second tower. It allowed me time to soak up the natural beauty of the area and to fully enjoy the marvel of the wall itself. I have never in my life felt so mortal and insignificant. The Great Wall of China was everything I could have possibly dreamed it would be and much more.

Needless to say, when we returned to the Beijing Radisson after our busy day of sightseeing, we were all exhausted—but we were also getting a bit antsy. Lorraine and I met Geoff and Melody, a couple from Topeka, KS, for dinner at the hotel restaurant. Geoff was very tall, more than six feet, bald, and sported a few tattoos. The first impression might make you cautious, but he was a super-nice guy with a big smile, and full of life. Melody was short in stature and side by side with Geoff looked even smaller. Geoff and Melody were very pleasant to be around, and Lorraine and I enjoyed their company.

Dinner was fantastic and the beer was cold, which we found to be an oddity. Finding any beverage cold in China was a rarity since it seemed, at least from our take, that it wasn't customary to drink anything that was cooler than room temperature. We ate and we drank and we toasted our children waiting in Nanchang. There were many questions hovering in our heads, so many that it was hard to sort them out, but we enjoyed sharing our life stories and our dossier experiences. One thing we found interesting about Geoff and Melody was that they didn't follow any blogs or any monthly updates other than the ones from Children's Hope. So when they got their referral, it was a total surprise. Lorraine and I were in awe of their patience and determination not to get so caught up during the waiting process.

Saturday was just about in the books and Sunday we were scheduled to leave Beijing and fly to the province of Jiangxi, to the city of Nanchang. This is where we would meet our daughter. It had been twenty-two months and seventeen days since we filed our dossiers, and now there were less than twenty-four hours between our daughter and the rest of our lives.

Sunday morning, I began to settle into a routine. I got up early, made a pot of coffee in the room for Lorraine, and then headed downstairs to the business center. I would update our Web site daily so our family could follow our journey. Once I had finished, I headed out on a walkabout around the hotel. The sights and sounds early in the morning, watching the people transport their produce and market merchandise on their bikes, scooters, and handcarts as they go rolling through the street toward the marketplace, is an eye-opening experience. The people of Beijing travel meticulously on their mission to provide for their families by selling fruit, vegetables, handwoven baskets, pearls, snakes, scorpions—all right, I think you get the picture. I was in a hypnotic trance watching all the early morning activity and thinking of what a grand day this would be for Lorraine and me. Our child was waiting in the province of Jiangxi and we would be there by 4 P.M. that afternoon. My mind wandered back and forth between the reality unfolding in front of me and our dream of finally holding our daughter, Samantha Jun.

Journal entry two

Leaving Beijing
Date: 06/23/2007

Yesterday we got to travel to Tiananmen Square and went through to the Forbidden City. It was amazing; we had no idea how huge it was. We just kept walking through a courtyard and a cluster of buildings and then another courtyard. It took about 2.5 hours to get all the way through and we didn't even really see everything. Then we took a bus ride to a nice Chinese restaurant and had our first sampling of Peking duck, which was very tasty. From there, we walked over to the Children's Hope offices and had an orientation about what to expect for the rest of our trip. Let me say again, our guide Elaine is just terrific. She has a fantastic sense of humor and really keeps us laughing, and she makes us all feel very secure because she is very knowledgeable and helpful.

From there we took an hour-long bus ride to a very famous spot on the Great Wall. To be honest, we were kind of tired and I was just ready to board the plane to Nanchang, but the wall was truly awe-inspiring. The countryside around it was mountainous with lots of greenery and it was just beautiful. Looking all around for miles, you could see glimpses of the wall. It's hard to describe the feeling we got. It was very humbling to know we were on a structure that was started before the birth of Jesus and continued for hundreds of years. Lorraine was able to make it to the second tower but too tired to get the certificate to prove it, plus I don't think she had any money. I had both the camera and the money and opted to climb about 3/4 of the way, then decided breathing was more important so decided to chat and take some awesome pictures. When we got back to the hotel, we showered and ran into one of the other couples downstairs and had a nice dinner with them. We leave in about 2 hours for Nanchang and we will meet our daughter tonight at 5 P.M. Even as I type this, I cannot believe it even though I've been planning her first outfit all week.

More to come . . .

The Great Wall of China (Beijing)

CHAPTER TWELVE

I HAD READ SOMEWHERE THAT a member of one of the previous traveling families had bought some U.S. postal stamps commemorating the Year of the Dog, and put them in small, clear Ziploc bags to hand out as gifts to the Chinese people. I thought that was such a cool idea and decided to do the same. I was able to acquire on eBay a sheet of U.S. stamps commemorating the Year of the Rabbit, and likewise packaged them in Ziploc bags to hand out as I was on my daily walkabouts. The bellboys and maid staff just loved me after receiving their stamps and seemed genuinely grateful. I felt like Santa Claus. I was having a blast and becoming well known to the hotel staff.

It was about 11:30 A.M. when we started boarding the bus headed toward the airport. I explained that Children's Hope pretty much took us by the hand and walked us through the whole process, and the in-country travel was no exception. The hotel room service picked up our bags from outside our door and delivered them to the airport.

Our bags were waiting for us when we arrived at Nanchang International Airport, loaded and ready to be put on our new tour bus. I have never seen such service in all my life. The luggage was picked up by the bell staff at the hotel. Because they picked up the group's luggage and transported the pieces to the airport together, we arrived in Nanchang to find that all the luggage had a sticky label with my last name on it. Everybody in the group asked me the same question: "Why is your name on my luggage?" I actually considered the possibility that

41

41

this was all part of the Chinese show, but if you think about it, it makes good sense. In America we are busy personalizing and individualizing everything, but in reality all the luggage was going to the same place, the same hotel, with the same group. It's actually very practical. We could probably take a lesson from it-another nice touch of showmanship.

The flight to Nanchang was not a good one for Lorraine, because our group had bought a mass of airline tickets, and in the confusion we did not sit together on the plane. Lorraine was paired with one of the more animated wives in the group, and it made for an interesting flight. I don't think Lorraine would have used the word *interesting*, but I'm writing this story. There was a Chinese gentleman sitting in the window seat of the row where she sat. This gentleman, listening to the boisterous vocals of this particular wife, complained to the stewardess. He rambled on in Chinese and the wife rambled on in English. I was three rows back and once again was extremely amused. Lorraine would give me the evil eye and I would try not to laugh.

The wait after we landed in Nanchang was excruciating. We had to wait for our luggage and then we were led by Elaine, Gloria, and Kate, our newest guide, who was a Nanchang native and expert. Interestingly, one of the families had brought along their four-year-old daughter, Tara, whom they had previously adopted from China. Her father was carrying her out to the bus and it was starting to drizzle. Some random guy ran over and held an umbrella over Tara's head until they got to the bus. In a sad kind of way, I believe the children were coveted more because of the government policy of one child only. The people of China knew these children would be leaving their homeland, and that it was probably forever.

Once we got on the bus, we had to wait again for the other two couples who had flown into Hong Kong. Their flight was slightly delayed, and I actually had to quiet my wife's grumbling about people not following the program. Of course, she got over this; it was just the anticipation of meeting our child that sidetracked her usual patience.

Finally, the bus was moving, and we had about a forty-five-minute ride before we got to the hotel. Everyone was filled with questions, and Kate patiently tried to answer them all. I remember Lorraine and me getting into a little tiff because she wanted to use the formula she had brought although everyone else was getting formula through our guides because that's what the babies were used to. My wife is a fanatic about nutrition, and the baby formula that the children were currently using was sweet smelling, almost like cake batter. You can understand why that didn't go over so easy; however, for the sake of our new baby, she eventually agreed to stick with what the baby was used to. Kate also took some time to tell us about the history and current information about Nanchang.

We had heard that there were several different ways that we could be receiving the babies. Some groups went straight to the orphanage or foster home, and sometimes the babies were brought to the hotel where the parents were staying. We listened intently as Kate told us that we would have to travel to the CCAA Civil Affairs office, where the orphanage staff would be meeting us with our babies. We were a little disappointed to hear that we would not get to see the orphanage where we thought our daughter had spent the first eight months of her life, but we felt really bad for the babies when Kate told us that they would be traveling for an hour on a bus with no air-conditioning to meet us. The poor babies would not have a clue what was going on.

Traveling through the city of Nanchang was a surreal experience. There was the appearance of this whole city with huge buildings. However, upon closer inspection, there were just all these large concrete buildings that were completely abandoned. Apparently, all of the structures had been started but funding ran out or something, so they just left these empty shells of buildings. It was really eerie looking, and unfortunately, it would also be the view from our hotel.

We finally arrived at the Glory Hotel, which was known to many as an "adoption hotel." It was a very old building, well decorated and clean, but you could see the obvious wear of all the years as you neared the entrance carport. It was known as one of the adoption hotels because all the international agencies used it when they had families adopting from the local orphanages. There were families from Spain and France in the hotel during that week, all getting their children and probably ending their journey in Guangzhou or wherever their countries' embassies were. Just for fun, Lorraine and I tried to keep a count on the families at the hotel with Chinese babies and children. We totaled 138 families, all there for the same reason. Keep in mind that this was one province and one city in China for that month. If you do the math, the numbers are staggering.

CHAPTER THIRTEEN

WE HAD AN HOUR TO wait before the bus would take us to our daughter. We were on pins and needles. Lorraine busied herself with unpacking; we barely spoke to each other. I just couldn't sit still and decided to go outside for a smoke. Finally, the tour bus that was going to take us to the Civil Affairs office arrived and all fourteen families (one family was still in another province and would meet up with us in Guangzhou) were in the lobby of the Glory eagerly awaiting the opportunity to board. This was it. Twenty-two months of waiting, crying, and more waiting were about to come to a head. Ready or not, here it comes.

I could see Elaine, Gloria, and Kate heading toward us with the Children's Hope flags in hand. We finally boarded the bus and the buzz was everywhere. I tried not to let it consume me but I was fooling nobody. Lorraine had become stoic and was lost in thought. I tried idle conversation, but I realized she was just soaking it all in. Kate began to set some ground rules that we needed to respect when we arrived at the Civil Affairs office. Chinese tradition is embedded with respect. It mostly involved not grabbing for the children. The nannies found this disrespectful. We were told to wait while you're waiting.

During our bus ride, Elaine and Kate spoke in turn about issues dealing with the China adoption program and the so-called one-child rule. I found the subjects interesting, but, similar to the history lessons we had received during our tours at the Great Wall and the

Forbidden City, there seemed to be a slight spin on the explanations and historical recollections. That's what drew me to conclude that we were being told what they wanted us to hear. I started to feel like we were being manipulated—not that it mattered in the long run, but you have to remember, the Chinese culture places great value in honor and appearances. Elaine's talk about China's one-child rule was interesting in that she explained the different ethnicities of China. The Han, Shang, Haung, and Chou clans are the largest groups and are allowed to have only one child. The upper social classes are actually allowed more than one but at a price. Education also determines how many children you can have, but for the majority of the people in China, it is pretty much law that you can have only one child. Not many can afford the high taxes that come with more than one child.

The social security system in China is basically the male children, because there is no governmental system in place for taking care of senior citizens. The custom is that when the sons of the families are grown, they marry and bring their wives to live in their parents' home. The sons inherit their family's belongings, including their parents to care for during their final years. This is one of the reasons why males are regarded as higher in value than females. Also, the farming families need the strength of the boys to help work in the fields.

They also talked about the CCAA's efforts to promote adoption domestically in China. It is a hard sell. Most Chinese are very concerned with bloodlines and family ties and are not willing to raise a child that is not biologically theirs. I thought it was interesting that when a child is adopted in China, it is kept very secret. No one outside the immediate family is told of the adoption, and the adopted child will probably never know that he or she is adopted. Another reason many Chinese families will not adopt is that they are expected to pay the same $3,000 orphanage donation the rest of us had to pay, and that is just not feasible for many families.

I gazed out the window of the tour bus and watched as we drove through the streets of Nanchang. The traffic was crazy. Pedestrians, bikes, and cars all intertwined, fighting for position, and it's amazing there aren't more accidents. It looked like a colony of worker ants scurrying back and forth at super-speed, going fast, but going nowhere. I watched in amazement as cars and pedestrians, pedestrians and bikes, motorbikes and cars just weaved in and out. No one seemed to be in a panic; it just seemed like another day at the office. I watched as we passed a Kentucky Fried Chicken, a McDonald's, and, to my surprise, a Wal-Mart.

The bus arrived and parked on a side street next to the Civil Affairs office. The ride was over; time to dismount! We began to pile out of the bus. It seemed like we were going forward in slow motion, like we were all in a dream-like state. I remember the small entrance, and that we had to go up the elevator in groups because the elevators were so small. Like most places that we visited in China, air-conditioning was a rarity, and the Civil Affairs building was no exception. The air was stagnant and it was very hot. I was wearing a T-shirt, shorts, and sandals, and I could tell I was hot because the sweat was dripping down my face and legs; however, I was barely aware of the discomfort.

We rode up the elevator with Tara and her parents. As the elevator began to move, someone asked the little girl if she was excited about meeting her little sister. She solemnly nodded and said, "And just because they're my toys doesn't mean I can't share." There was a brief break from the tension as her comment made everyone smile.

The elevator doors slid open and I remember walking into a large room. I can't remember hearing anything, even though I could see babies screaming, mouths wide open, but no sound. I looked at Lorraine and saw that she was searching the room for Samantha. We knew we couldn't approach the babies, but we were dying just to see her face. I continued my search, and it seemed that as I became more frantic and desperate, the noise began to filter through, and it continued until all I could hear was screaming. Lorraine would look at me and shake her head as if to say, "I can't find her." Other families were tripping over us and each other, all looking for a daughter they knew only from a picture. I passed Geoff and Melody several times, and we tried to comfort each other by joking about the screaming children—"That's probably my daughter screaming her head off"—and then moving on as we continued the search.

Lorraine thought she had spotted Samantha, but it was wishful thinking. This baby sat by herself and was all smiles. This was not to be our fate!

While Lorraine and I endured the grueling wait for our referral, our imaginations took control. We had fantasized how it would be meeting Samantha for the first time, and it was a vision more or less like a Hollywood production. We didn't see ourselves running through an open field or anything that mundane, but we did expect some kind of fanfare. In one scenario, we saw ourselves being called to a private room by a smiling yet tearful nanny as our child was presented to us. We were in for the shock of our lives. This wasn't a fairy-tale ending; this was more like a B mystery movie with a wicked plot.

I had fooled myself into believing that this was the day, the day I get to hold my daughter, the day I get to see her face and feel her touch, the day I have anticipated for nearly two years. No one, and I mean no one, could derail this dream! I was mistaken. There was no fanfare. There were no streamers or balloons; there was nothing to indicate that something special was happening on this day. There was just a room full of strangers lining the room, each holding two or three screaming babies, while we stood helplessly in the middle of it all.

Chapter Fourteen

ALL THE CHILDREN HAD NAMETAGS with pictures hanging around their necks, but it didn't seem to help Lorraine and I locate Samantha. We watched as others began receiving their babies, and I began to notice that the screams were getting louder. Reality was creeping in, and I was starting to see the whole picture. I continued looking and had completely searched the room. There was only one child whose face I couldn't see because a Chinese man was holding her in some form of headlock. I was fuming to think that it might be Samantha. In hindsight, I realize this poor man was just trying to maneuver and keep a grip on three other children, but it was the one child he had in a headlock that drew my interest. Could that be her? Little by little, as the other families began receiving their babies, it was obvious to me that that screaming child in the headlock was my poor Samantha. Just then, I heard them call out our name. It was time, and I watched as an older Chinese lady scooped up Samantha from the Chinese man holding on to her head and brought her to us. I was in shock!

I thought I was prepared for anything and everything by this point, but I was soon to realize I was nowhere near ready for what was to come next. Lorraine and I literally ran to where Elaine and Samantha were standing and waiting. We carried all of our identification and legal papers so they could match Samantha to us by names. They were just making sure this child was the one they had promised. They looked at our paperwork, matched it with the tag around Samantha's neck, handed her over to Lorraine, and moved on to the next in line. The child was totally flushed from crying and seemed to have a cold or the flu, but she did stop crying after Lorraine held her close in her arms. She was probably in shock, too! Lorraine passed Samantha to me, and at that time, I knew only one thing to be true: I was a happy man!

I couldn't hold back the tears, and I couldn't stop kissing her cheek. Nothing at this point mattered. But as the initial joy began to subside, I started to look closely at Samantha, and the first obvious thing I noticed was that she was very congested with mucus. She actually rattled when she breathed. Her little Mohawk was gone, and she was pasty white. The next thing I noticed was the shape of her head. I can laugh now, but I didn't find the humor in it at the time. Her head was flat and thin, sort of like a Nutter Butter peanut butter cookie. It was round when you looked at the front of it, but thin when you turned it. It would take four months of wearing a head helmet to correct this damage. To make her head look even odder, she had hair only on the top of her head; the back was just bald. I wasn't prepared for that, but it really concerned me that she was so congested. I just wanted to get her back to the hotel, change her out of the funky outfit she had on, bathe her, and get her clean so I could kiss her on her face without making myself look like a glazed doughnut.

We had been told we would be able to talk to Samantha's caregivers and get information on her feeding and sleeping schedule, her likes and dislikes, and so forth. Maybe we weren't aggressive enough in seeking anyone out, but no one approached us, either. It was a chaotic scene and we were completely engrossed in our child. Then, they had to move our group out to bring the next group in. We ended up leaving that office with no extra information, just Samantha and the clothes on her back.

CHAPTER FIFTEEN

IN CHINA, IT IS ILLEGAL to put your child up for adoption, making abandoning your baby the only painful option for young mothers who either can't care for their babies or are pressured by their husbands and families to give their daughters up. Of course, it is also illegal to abandon the babies, and China being a communist country, I can only imagine that the law delivers a harsh punishment to those who are caught. In the area where we believe Samantha was born, they were mostly poor farming people. To these poor folks who barely eke out a living, such fines and penalties would be impossible to pay and could even mean imprisonment.

We also learned from Elaine that there is no government health care system in China. So if a baby is born with any kind of deformity or serious health problems, whether it's a boy or a girl, their mother is forced to abandon them. It is just too much of a financial burden for most of these families to care for a special-needs child.

We'd like to think, and it does makes sense, that there are unwritten rules known to the majority about where to leave these babies so that they are sure to be found quickly by the nannies who work at the orphanages.

On the flip side, I had also read somewhere that there is a river near an orphanage where mothers leave their babies. Should they encounter another baby occupying that spot, the mother will usually drown that baby to give her own baby a better chance of being rescued. What an unthinkable, crude, and primitive display of love; it makes you wonder how things became so dire. It's hard to imagine how anyone, regardless of the "why," could become so coldhearted and dark. Although I thought I understood the power of a parent's love, my heart breaks knowing these things could actually be true!

It was an interesting ride back to the hotel after filing out of the adoption center. Everyone was preoccupied with their babies, and the mood was mutual for all the families who now held their bundles of joy. We had been told that the babies were used to drinking their bottles scalding hot and that they were not used to air-conditioning. I wasn't thrilled when they told us to keep our rooms warm, but I certainly saw the necessity of it, because Samantha had never been exposed to air-conditioning. As we were instructed, we wrapped Samantha in a blanket for the bus ride to our hotel. I looked at her face and could see the curiosity, and I wondered what was going through her mind as she sat there being loved up by two complete strangers. This look of curiosity stayed with her for the next three days. It was a rather stoic look, and at times, it was unnerving because it was a stare that seemed to go right through you as though she was sizing us up.

We sat there on the bus forgetting at times there were thirteen other families there, too; we were lost in our own little world. Lorraine and I were eager to get back to the hotel and get Samantha bathed and changed out of her smelly little split-pants outfit. I read somewhere that these babies are usually potty trained by the time they are six to eight months old. Babies who are not able to sit up on their own are enclosed in a wooden box up to the neck to hold them in place. As Americans, we found this practice simply unthinkable.

Samantha was a bit stinky, but I knew I was in love with this precious little girl, and I knew water and soap would solve the stinky problem. We needed to get back to the hotel, and it needed to be now!

Elaine and Kate again took turns giving instructions or giving us details of events to happen in the next few days to complete the process here in Nanchang and prepare us for our final stop in Guangzhou. Nobody was listening! We had several important appointments in the next few days that we had to prepare for as part of the process. There was paperwork that needed to be filled in and signed that night by both parents saying we would accept the baby, and we were limited on time. We had left the hotel around 4 P.M. and it was now almost 8 P.M. We had to get back to our room and take care of the baby, and then Lorraine and I would have to take turns watching her as we each went down to the meeting room to sign the necessary forms. There was still much to do, and we were again feeling overwhelmed.

It was unusual for me to take the reins and run the show, but while we were in China, that's exactly what happened. I became the moneyman, the packer, the coordinator for the appointments, and the positive influence on everything we did in China. I followed the itinerary to the letter, I listened to our Children's Hope representative as to where we needed to be and at what time, and I handled all the money situations. This allowed Lorraine to just concentrate on Samantha. I got to do my part in that, too, but it seemed I was most valuable at seeing to all the details. It was a complete role reversal for us, and it shows how close we are in our friendship and trust. We make one heck of a team!

CHAPTER SIXTEEN

WE ARRIVED AT THE HOTEL, where everybody exited the bus and headed for the elevators to get to their rooms to bond with and inspect the babies.

Once we were enclosed in our room, we quickly removed Samantha's clothes, and, even faster, discarded them in the trash. Lorraine went to start the bathwater, and I began the inspection. I removed Samantha's socks and found an address label stuck on her foot. I thought nothing about it at the time, but for whatever reason, I kept that label safe in my wallet. It would prove to be very helpful later.

After fully inspecting Samantha from her head (a rather thin head) to her toes, my only concern was the rattling of mucus in her chest. It seemed to hamper her when she was feeding from her bottle, because she really couldn't breathe through her nose. Lorraine had finished running the bathwater, and together we bathed Samantha. It was really more of a sponge bath, because she was so ill that Lorraine was worried about causing her additional impairment.

We spent the next several hours lying on the bed staring at Samantha and taking turns running downstairs to the lobby to sign paperwork. At eight months old, Samantha couldn't hold her head up when we lifted her from the bed. She was like a newborn in that respect. She also could not sit up. We had understood that babies born and raised in orphanages would be developmentally behind, so we were not too concerned or shocked at these revelations. We knew with a lot of attention and TLC, she would catch up quickly.

What Lorraine and I were most concerned about was Samantha's medical condition. Her congestion made her every breath sound desperate and difficult. We were in for a long night!

There was one saving grace for Samantha in that we were able to provide antibiotics for her. In talking to other families in our group, we found that some had asked their doctors for antibiotics but were turned down. We'd caught a break because my regular physician had a sister who had just adopted from China, so he had given us antibiotics and several other medicines to combat against anything young babies might generally need at this early stage. Lorraine and I had debated for weeks about administering the antibiotics. I had wanted to start Samantha on them no matter what, and she thought we should wait and see if she actually needed them because she didn't want Samantha to build immunity to them. Well, seeing Samantha's condition put an end to that debate. We immediately started her on the medicine. I had to place my trust in the medicine and my prayers, because that was all I had to give her.

The hotel had provided a "crib," but it looked more like a sled or a wooden pallet with no mattress—just a thick comforter-type blanket. There was no way we were letting Samantha sleep on that thing. I had heard these children were accustomed to sleeping on hard beds, but not on my watch! We leaned the sled against a far wall out of our way and made up the second twin bed for Samantha and surrounded her lower body with pillows. We felt safe doing this because she was still so much like a very young baby and not very mobile at all.

Lorraine and I stayed on the other twin bed and kept a vigil over Samantha all night. I found myself creeping over to her throughout the night and looking for signs that she was still breathing. I don't mean to sound melodramatic, but we were scared for her life. We had planned on rotating shifts, but neither of us could sleep.

The hotel maid service eventually figured out we weren't going to use the pallet they had provided as a crib and after a few days stopped putting the pallet back on the floor. It's funny how Lorraine and I squeezed into the other twin bed, but I think it was God's way of telling me I needed to hold her and reassure her during this time of uncertainty, and I think Lorraine appreciated it.

"Tough First Night" Nanchang Jiangxi

Journal entry three

Samantha Day

Date: 06/24/2007

We arrived in Nanchang and went to the Gloria Hotel. We all met again in the lobby and drove by bus to the adoption center to meet the babies. It was unlike any experience I have ever witnessed, both good and sad. The families all meeting their children, well, there was not a dry eye in the house. Samantha was beautiful. We didn't stay there long after the exchange so as to give all the families time to spend and bond with their new child. There was also another group on the way up, which, too, pressed us for time. It wasn't exactly the romantic intro to Samantha I spent two years dreaming of, hence the sad part; it was more of a lackluster event. I say that not so much for how I felt, but in the attitudes of the Chinese. It reminded me of my enlisted days in the army, sort of an issuing of uniforms and weapons situation. I apologize for the blunt description, but it was very surreal and I wanted to remain as honest as possible since this is being recorded for Samantha's benefit! Anyway, Samantha was very congested so we started her on the antibiotics that the Dr. gave us and she seems better this morning. We have a busy day today doing a lot of the legal stuff, but all is well and we could not be any happier! I can't wait for everyone to meet her. More info to come soon!

Lorraine and I actually woke up a few minutes before Samantha the following morning, and Lorraine hopped into the shower. I proceeded to get the morning bottle ready. By the time Lorraine came back to the room, Samantha was awake and proceeded to drink the whole eight-ounce bottle. Lorraine was telling me how great Samantha's appetite was and how great that she was able to drink down a whole bottle. She then stood up and put Samantha on her shoulder so she could burp her. Samantha proceeded to spew that whole eight ounces of milk right into Lorraine's hair and down her back. "Welcome to motherhood!" I said, laughing. After a scalding look from Lorraine, I took Samantha so my wife could hop back into the shower.

Samantha seemed a tad bit better, but she was not out of the woods. This may sound gross and disgusting, but her mucus was yellow and stringy, which usually means an infection, and we soon discovered that she had a double ear infection. I'd never seen anything so tricky to work with. Samantha, just like most children, really didn't care for anybody wiping her face, so it made for a sticky situation, no pun intended. The thing that amazed me more than anything else was her ability to tolerate all of her ailments and concentrate on trying to figure out just who we were and why she was with us.

After Lorraine finished redressing, she took Samantha, and I ran downstairs to find the Glory Hotel's business center and update our Web site so our family and friends could see where we were in the process. Our family was eager to see the first photo of us holding Samantha.

Crib (pallet) at the Glory Hotel

CHAPTER SEVENTEEN

ON THIS DAY WE WERE scheduled to process more paperwork, which meant another road trip. I found it so funny that as we loaded the bus to attend to the business side of the adoption—such as the notary office and a repeat visit to the Civil Affairs office—the main topic of conversation was whether or not the babies had had a bowel movement. It seemed that the Children's Hope representatives knew that the sudden change in environment would affect these babies' schedules. Samantha had not had a bowel movement yet that morning. Elaine mentioned that if they didn't have a bowel movement soon, there was always the "Chinese way." I didn't know what that was, but I prayed extra hard for Samantha to do it the natural way.

During the times between our departures and arrivals to the different locations, Elaine would tell us stories and give us information that was pertinent to where we were going. I really think this helped take the edge off some of the new experiences we were going to face. It also helped relax everyone, to the degree we were capable of relaxing, considering why we were all in China in the first place. One of the stories that Elaine told us tugged my heartstrings so much, I found myself trying to fight back the tear that wanted to roll down my cheek. Elaine was not a newcomer in the adoption process for Children's Hope. She was experienced, and unlike Gloria had witnessed the exchange many times, but she said she never grew tired of it. She told us that it was not always so.

On Elaine's first trip with Children's Hope, they had given her a small group of seven families, and as is Children's Hope's custom, she had walked them through the whole process. However, she said, because it was her first time, her English was dreadful. I didn't find it to be that much better this time around either, but she began tell us about her first assignment and how she thought it had gone rather well. At the end of each assignment, families involved are asked by their agencies to rate the treatment and care received from their agency representatives. All seven families complained that they could not understand Elaine's English and that it made things very difficult at times. Elaine was very disappointed—so much so that she told Children's Hope she was going to resign. Children's Hope asked Elaine to give it one more try and said that if she felt the same after her next assignment, they would accept her resignation.

Elaine's second assignment started roughly the same as her first. There seemed to be no major problems or issues, and she still thought she was going to resign after the assignment was over. It was a glitch in the final family's plight that sent her world reeling and set her mood about her role with Children's Hope forever.

Elaine's second group had a family that was expedited because they had chosen to adopt an older child, and that family was able to go to the orphanage where their child was living. Elaine told our group that as they arrived, the orphanage children were performing a play in honor of a nationally celebrated Chinese holiday. Elaine waited patiently while the child in question did her part in the play. While she was waiting with the new parents, another young child came and asked her why she was waiting for this one child. Elaine told her that she had found her parents, and that they were there to take her home. The young child didn't miss a beat and asked Elaine, "Can you find my parents for me?" It was a pivotal moment in Elaine's life.

China's one-child policy has met much criticism from the people of China, and Elaine realized that because the law would most likely be in place for years to come, it would be in her country's best interest if people like her made sure that the future of the abandoned children was secured. Elaine felt she had found her purpose. This story brought everybody on the bus to tears, but more important, I for one am glad she was part of our journey!

Our first stop was back at the Civil Affairs office, where we had picked up Samantha the day before. We opted to take turns wearing Samantha in a front carrier to keep her close, and, we hoped, to help her bond to us—Lorraine and I were already there.

We had a lackluster interview with a very young Chinese woman whose attitude resembled that of a government worker in America. The office that she occupied was small, but the desk where she sat was humongous, which made her look even younger. We stood in line and waited our turn. It seemed like the families before us were in and out in two to three minutes. I was curious what this process was supposed to accomplish. Our turn to enter the office had arrived, and we went in and sat down. Then came part of what I called the "show" again. The young lady was very stoic looking and stared right through us as she asked, "Are you happy with this child?" and "Do you promise to never abandon this child?" I so wanted to be a smart-ass, but I knew this was not the venue. Lorraine and I said, "Yes, we are happy with this child and we promise to never abandon this child," and then we were dismissed. It had a callous and impersonal feel to it, kind of like taking a test at the Department of Motor Vehicles back home.

We proceeded to walk down the hall and gave a gentleman behind a pane of thick Plexiglas our $1,100 for various legal and administrative fees. We got a receipt and were back in the hallway. It seemed rather pointless, but I guess maybe the CCAA thought it needed to justify the fee amount we had just paid. I don't know, but if it was the Chinese administration's way of mitigating the fee, I could have done without the forged fanfare.

We were actually able to wire the $3,000 orphanage donation before our travel; it was nice to be able to check that off our "to do" list before we left the country. Not all provinces offered this luxury, and I don't know what the procedure would have been for that transaction. It would have felt very strange to hand the orphanage director $3,000 in cash right after they handed us our daughter.

Our next stop was a short bus ride away to the notary office to sign a document and give another gift. The notary actually gave us a warm smile and made us feel human again. We actually felt some acknowledgment from him that this was a special time for us.

I remember exchanging gifts with the orphanage director on the previous day. He had given us a beautiful carved wooden dragon with the province's name as a keepsake for Samantha. The notary gave us a fancy porcelain knickknack holder of some sort, but the rest of the exchanges came from my rear pant pocket. Some of the fees averaged in the thousands, but all in all, it was what we expected and there were no surprises.

There was one more stop to get pictures made for the babies' passports, and then it was back to the Glory.

I had become a pal to one of the sons traveling with his parents to get their daughter and his sister. I felt bad for him since at eleven years old, he had no one his age to hang with, and for some reason, he took to me like a duck to water. I remember his parents telling me that they thought for a moment that they might have picked up my camera since there were so many pictures of me on it! Their son was just lost in the big scheme of it all and tried to occupy himself as best he could. He was a good kid.

We spent the evening back at the hotel. Just inside the main doors was a small lounge, and we joined a few of the families there to talk about the day's events and share stories about our new babies. A short time later, we went back to our room to order up some room service, and Lorraine ordered a BLT. Interestingly enough, it had egg on it. This was another interesting little twist on Americanized food, and we were to learn that it was a recurring theme.

When we finished our meal, we focused completely on Samantha. Lorraine had packed a few little stuffed animals and rattles for her. She took them out and put them in front of Samantha. Samantha looked at the toys and then looked at us like, "What the heck am I supposed to do with that?" We shook the rattles and snuggled the stuffed animals up to her, but she just wasn't interested.

We decided to set the toys aside and just carried her around the room and watched the city from our window. We had a great view of the river and all the barges and small boats going back and forth. We got to watch a very busy intersection and held our breath at some of the maneuvers we saw people making. Across the street from the hotel were buildings, one of which had a neon sign that stayed lighted from around midnight until about 3 A.M. that read "Foot Massage." One of the men in our group told a story about how he had gone to one of these places for a foot massage and how they had asked him what else he wanted.

Across the river was the vacant city we'd seen on the way in. As we stared out the window, we saw some rain clouds rolling in fast. Within minutes, a vicious storm was raining down on us, and suddenly our window was leaking. As I frantically gathered towels to soak up the water, my wife called the front desk to report the leak. She threw her hands up in frustration when the operator told her, "Just the close the window." Of course, our window was closed and we laughed about it later, but at the time, we just weren't in the mood.

After Samantha fell asleep, we gathered some clothes for the laundry service. Lorraine was actually a little giddy when we got our laundry back the next morning, neatly folded and presented to us in wicker baskets.

In those first few days after we had received our children, each family spent hours and hours creating a bond between them and their child. Most of the families bonded almost immediately, but one couple with a one-year-old child who had been in a foster home was having attachment issues. At the Glory, most of us were on the same floor of the hotel and the walls were thin. We were next to this couple's room, and for those first few days, their child cried constantly and inconsolably. I know this must have been unnerving and gut wrenching for them. By the second day, she had bonded with her dad, and by the end of the trip, she seemed to have bonded with both parents equally. Again, we were thankful that Samantha was younger, making the bonding process a little easier for us.

The next day was a free day and our leaders scheduled a visit to the local Wal-Mart. It was unlike any Wal-Mart I'd ever seen. Lorraine and I had to pick up some of the same formula that our leaders had given us. We had been forewarned that the Chinese people in Wal-Mart might come up to see the babies. I didn't mind the people who came with big smiles who just wanted to see the pretty baby, but we also got what felt like hostile stares, which made me uneasy. I tried to empathize; I can only imagine what I would be feeling as I witnessed a bunch of foreigners coming to our homeland and taking our children, regardless the situation. I sort of understood, but it didn't make the situation any easier. I remember my wife commenting under her breath, "Don't be mad at us for taking your babies—you should have taken better care of them yourselves!" My usually congenial wife was turning into quite the tiger now that she was a mother. It was hard for both of us to stomach the thought of the inadequate care and attention these precious babies had been receiving.

Anyway, back to Wal-Mart. It was a four-story building surrounded by local merchant shops selling all kinds of watches, jade jewelry, pearl necklaces and bracelets, and unique Chinese souvenirs. This Wal-Mart was an extraordinary place! The shopping carts were much smaller compared with those in America. There were devices on the wheels of the carts that looked like suction cups, and all four wheels rotated. This made the buggies hard to steer. Our leaders took us to the fourth floor, since that's where all the baby stuff was.

Lorraine and I picked up the essentials we needed and decided to explore the store a little more thoroughly. We circled the fourth floor and at first couldn't figure out how to move to the next floor. Then we saw what looked like an escalator with no steps. This is where the suction-cup-looking devices came in. As you load onto the flat escalator, these suction cups are actually magnets that attach themselves to the metal slats so that the buggy hooks on and you ride it down or up to the next floor. Once you reach the end of the escalator, the magnets release and off you go. It was absolutely amazing! The next few floors were full of clothing and small appliances. The food level was very interesting with all the different types of canned food for that region. I was pretty surprised to see that beer and liquor were sold in the Wal-Mart. The meat department had live-eel tanks, shark fins and steaks, scorpions, turtles, and some other forms of dead animal flesh that I didn't recognize—and it was probably better that way.

I went looking for some deodorant and was sporting Samantha in our front-facing carrier. I was clueless and staring at all the products on this particular shelf and noticed some of the Chinese patrons staring and pointing at me with a giggle on their faces. I looked back on the shelf and realized I was so focused on finding the deodorant, I hadn't even noticed that the products on the shelves were sexually oriented goods. I was so embarrassed that I scurried away, looking down so as to not make eye contact with my ridiculers.

After our rather interesting trip to Wal-Mart, our leaders offered to stop at McDonald's, and most everyone on the bus gave an enthusiastic "Yeah!" I really don't remember what we got—I think just some French fries—but someone on the bus got the burger with, you guessed it, egg on it.

Back at the hotel, we headed back up to our room to relax for a little while. We had Samantha sitting up on the bed propped up between two pillows. We were amazed that even though she was so congested, it did not seem to hamper her from staring at everything and taking in everything around her. We had been playing with her constantly, and although she was fully engaged with us, she would not crack a smile. We figured, why would she smile or laugh when she can hardly breathe? I was caressing Samantha's head and rubbing her cheeks, mostly to feel her temperature since she hated the thermometer, when I accidentally rubbed my finger across her armpit and little biceps muscle. I saw a grin from her that covered her face ear to ear, so I tried it again. This time I actually tried to tickle her. Samantha busted out with such a hearty laugh, that once again Lorraine and I cried. We had become crybabies during our trip in China, and I'll admit we've carried some of that home. It was such an emotional roller-coaster ride, and our emotions sometimes took us by surprise.

It wasn't until that evening as we were winding down in our room after a brief foray to the lounge that we noticed something about Samantha that to this day still holds true. She's a dancer! Samantha loves music and will dance to almost anything. We had the TV on, but unfortunately China television leaves much to be desired when you don't speak the language. The only program on the set was some form of Chinese MTV music video program. However, it was actually during a commercial that James Brown hit the airwaves with "Get Up Offa That Thing," and Lorraine almost took my breath away with an elbow as she tried to get my attention. Samantha suddenly started rocking back and forth, side to side, with some sort of hand motion. It was the cutest thing to see. Lorraine and I sat and watched her, and we laughed and we cried and the tears of joy rolled down our cheeks.

Samantha had danced and laughed, overcoming how bad she must have felt. I really believe it was her strong will that saved Lorraine and me from going crazy. She made us laugh, and she made us cry.

We knew then beyond any doubts that this was our child. Anyone who knows Lorraine and me knows how important music is to us. It's always been a large part of our lives. So the fact that Samantha obviously was into music and really felt it—I can hardly find the words. Samantha would do many little things in the few days that would warm our hearts, but Lorraine and I will always remember her first dance. In fact, for the next several days, Lorraine or I were able to get Samantha to duplicate her dance simply by singing, "Get up offa that thing, and dance till you feel better!"

Unfortunately, that night was a rough one for Samantha. She woke up almost every hour crying out. We were up and down all night and finally just got out of bed at 5 A.M. After Samantha had her bottle, we decided to go on downstairs for some breakfast. The restaurant was still closed so we decided to wait around in the lounge. Lorraine had to walk around with Samantha because that was the only thing that kept her from crying.

Across the lobby, we saw a Chinese man and his son approaching the restaurant. They were openly staring at us, but the man at least kept smiling and nodding. They, too, saw that the restaurant was closed and turned back to look at us. As he approached, I remember thinking, Here we go again! It turns out that the Chinese gentleman was an American citizen from, of all places, Alabama. He was in China with his son. He wanted his son to see where he came from and understand his cultures and traditions. I found him fascinating. The first thing he said to us was "You're doing God's work." He felt we were doing the Christian thing and just beamed at us. I found this comforting since he was a Chinese native. Up until that point, I had felt that the attitude was just the opposite of what this gentleman was expressing. I know now that God's hand was involved, but at that moment I wasn't expecting any support from the Chinese, especially while we were in Nanchang. His sentiment hit me hard, but I received it in the spirit I know he meant for it to be. He loved playing with Samantha and was just enthralled with her. Alabama—go figure.

Our tour guides and Children's Hope representatives tried to keep us busy, and you know, we didn't really appreciate it so much the first few days. However, by this time, more families began to get stir-crazy and wanted to venture out to sightsee. After breakfast that morning, our group went to visit Teng Wang Pavilion. It was a short walk from our hotel, and we were all enthusiastic about not having to load back onto the bus.

The pavilion was built in A.D. 653, when the Teng Wang (King) Li Yuanying, a younger brother of the Emperor Taizong of Teng dynasty, was the governor of Hong Zhou (now Nanchang). The nine-story pavilion, with its special charm of green tiles and double-eave roof, is now attracting guests from all over the world. The top floor of the pavilion held a stage for dancers to give a tribute to Emperor Tiazong that was presented every few hours.

We were watching the dancers perform when a group of men jumped in front of us, blocking the view. An elderly Chinese lady looked at Samantha and pushed the group of men back, telling them in Chinese that the baby couldn't see and for them to move back. At least that's what I think, since I don't speak Chinese. But it was pretty obvious what had transpired from the body language and these ladies fussing over Samantha. I found that odd and interesting!

As interesting and as beautiful as this pavilion was, we could not help but be reminded that the temperature outside was 104 degrees and inside the pavilion was almost unbearable, especially with a small child strapped to you. The Chinese custom of urinating outside on the balcony corners didn't help much either. We saw cleaning women constantly struggling to scrub the corners of the outside balcony clean. So although we were game for a little while, the heat and the smell of urine eventually got to us and we straggled back to the hotel lobby.

I'm sure the hotel staff got a chuckle out of how these Americans would leave the hotel, fresh, dry, every hair in place, every crease ironed and smelling good and fresh, only to return two hours later, hair stuck to our heads, clothes soaked and stuck to our bodies, babies crying and smelling like last week's wash. We must have been a sight!

We took Samantha straight up to our room and gave her a bottle of water and juice for the first time. She sucked that down in just a few minutes and conked out for a long nap. We took that opportunity to order a pizza from the local Pizza Hut and have some lunch. The pizza fortunately did not have egg on it and wasn't too bad.

We decided to head down to the lounge when Samantha woke up, and we ran into a few of the other families and sat and hung out for a little while. Again, it seemed that the more time we spent with these families, the more we spotted the resemblances between the couples and their new babies. There was one couple from New York who joined us frequently in the lounge. The wife had a head full of curly hair and big, expressive eyes. Their daughter had the biggest head of hair in the group, and she had her mother's eyes.

While we were talking, Lorraine was holding Samantha and decided to try tossing her in the air. With tears in her eyes, Lorraine passed Samantha to me and said, "You gotta try this." I took her, and after a few tosses and seeing Samantha's big grin, I had tears of my own. With the conversation going on around us, I squeezed Samantha tight and Lorraine and I stared into each other's teary eyes and grinned. These were the special moments that make me miss our time in the lounge of the Glory Hotel.

At 3 P.M., a group of us gathered and walked across the street to a little shop called Tiffany's. We had heard we could have a traditional dress made for Samantha and knew we had to have one. As we walked into the tiny shop, we saw they had many ready-made Chinese outfits as well, and we decided to pick up a few for Lorraine's niece and nephew. When it was our turn to talk about the dress we wanted custom-made, we realized that the Chinese have cornered the market on capitalism! They are kings of the up-sell. Before we knew it, we had bought a dress, a pants suit, and a scroll with Samantha's Chinese and American names on it.

After that dizzying experience, we went back to our rooms to just hang out with Samantha. Spending two weeks in a foreign country was not easy, but the time we got to spend with our new baby was priceless. We didn't have to go to work; we had no housework, laundry, or yard work to take up our time. For those two straight weeks, we spent every waking minute getting introduced to our new daughter. It was brilliant! We would joke that Samantha believed we lived in a hotel and always traveled in packs. But I'll tell you, before we began our trip back home, our baby answered to her name and knew we belonged to her.

I liked to sit by the window of our hotel room and watch the traffic below. I would be stunned at the sights and sounds of this particular intersection. I remember around 5 P.M., a brave or maybe a suicidal policeman would actually direct traffic from the center of the intersection. This was much better than television. I was fascinated by the congestion and near misses, the pedestrians trying to cross, the bicycle riders heading through traffic in the wrong direction, and the bus drivers forcing their way in between cars, bikes, and pedestrians. It was a sight to see!

Because the previous night had seemed pretty traumatic for Samantha, I let Lorraine have the twin bed all to herself, and I slept with Samantha on the other twin bed. It must have worked, because she slept all the way through the night to 5 A.M.

Journal entry four

Day 4 Nanchang
Date: 06/27/2007

Samantha is improving every day. Her motor skills and development are a little behind. She is 8 months yesterday and she has the motor skills of a 4 month old. She can't hold her head up on her own, she doesn't reach for things and will not put anything in her mouth, but she is becoming more active and more trusting each day. She smiles at us and will reach out to us, and now she is even blessing us with baby talk. It is absolutely adorable! Today we are going to the village to see a poor side of Nanchang and the people here say it is a lesson in humility. It is very hot here. The heat index is around 104 degrees and the humidity is 98%. It's sauna-like at best. Tonight is our last night here, because tomorrow they will issue us Samantha's passport and we will leave Friday evening to Guangzhou. More to come later …
Love
Carlos, Lorraine, and Samantha

Teng Weng Pavilion

Teng Weng Pavilion

CHAPTER EIGHTEEN

IT WAS HUMOROUS HOW THE Chinese were able to translate English to justify their jokes. Everyone in our Children's Hope group knew a few mundane Chinese phrases and words, but none of us were fluent enough to get more than directions to the toilets, and even then we weren't sure that's what we were asking for. Lorraine and I tried learning to say, "I love you" in Chinese, but sad to say, we were afraid Samantha had never heard those words and wouldn't understand anyway. I mention the humor of the language because our Children's Hope representative, as we traveled and toured in the bus, would tell us jokes. The English translations were always a bit skewed and if told correctly were not funny because they were bad interpretations of English words. Example: Why did the bicycle have to stop and rest? Because it was too tires (*tired* was the word they had incorrectly translated and pronounced). Needless to say, our guides found this joke hysterical. Although all the Americans on the bus were struggling to find the humor, we stayed cordial and did the courtesy smile at them. Elaine had the best joke while we were sightseeing (even though it was also an exploitation of English) about how it was a custom in China that there are three rings involved during courtship and marriage: engagement ring, wedding ring, and suffering.

Our Children's Hope representatives, Kate, Elaine, and Gloria, had planned for us to take a trip on Thursday to the porcelain market in Nanchang with a special stop at "the village." Nanchang, as we

71

discovered, was known for its beautiful and delicate handcrafted porcelain. The day started out as usual, with all the families loading in the bus around 9 A.M., and we were off to the village. There was times when the language barrier did seem to affect Lorraine and me, and we were unsure what they had said the plan was for this day, but we knew we wanted to get out of the hotel for a spell.

Kate did most of the talking during our ride to the village. I had up to this point believed we were being manipulated in the sense that they showed us what they wanted us to see and told us what they wanted us to hear, so I considered this another round of propaganda. Kate told stories and bad jokes on the trip to our next stop. As it turned out, "the village" was the extremely poor section of the city. It was a lesson in humility for some, but I had grown up poor, so I was not as shocked as some of the other families. We were told that villages like this were where most of our babies had come from. At first, Lorraine told me she did not feel comfortable getting off the bus. She said that to her, it would be like a tour bus stopping in the ghetto so we could see how low these people live. In the end, she did walk through the village because she felt that it would be important to share with Samantha one day.

One of the husbands had brought a bag of candy to give the children. I had told him to be careful because these kids weren't going to line up in an orderly manner while he passed out the candy and patted them on the head. Sure enough, as soon as he stepped off that bus wielding the bag of candy, a mob of kids arrived out of nowhere. They almost had him to the ground when he did the smart thing and let go of the bag. It seemed to surprise and alarm everyone, but the children were mostly harmless. They were just deprived of these types of goodies. They had learned that when the tour buses pulled up, they were getting treats and it was every man for himself. I admit, I was slightly amused, but I kept my "I told you so" to myself.

I found out later that the children took the entire batch of gifts, candy, sports cards, and American souvenirs to the village elders. There was a system in place, and they all adhered to it.

As we walked through the village, we saw just children and old people. All of the younger adults were in the fields working. One of the older ladies followed our group smiling, and when we got to what was apparently her house, she invited us in to take a look. It was a cinder-block house connected to a row of cinder-block houses. The floor was dirt, but it was swept clean, and her little home was very clean as well. Kate pointed to some newer buildings that the government was adding on. It definitely felt staged because it certainly felt like these people were expecting us, and I'm sure many groups had traveled through this village before us.

I did have an interesting experience that happened during our visit to the village. As we turned the corner to come back down a row of houses, we saw one boy who seemed like the bully of the group. He had returned after giving up all his goodies to the elders and was carrying three ears of cooked corn. I have several tattoos on my shoulders and biceps, which most Chinese found interesting. The young bully would run up from behind me and slap my biceps on the largest of my tattoos. He would circle around and slap my arm several times as we made our way throughout the village tour.

Several young girls in the group of village children seemed to just follow and remain low-key during the tour, and I made it a point to hand them each one of my U.S. postal stamps. I had several left and I gave them each one, which they took with a warm giggle before scampering off. I guessed the elders would eventually gain possession of these stamps, but it still warmed my heart to see their faces glow when I gave them the gifts.

The tour was over, and we were heading back to the bus when I saw the little bully. It seemed he was bragging to his entourage about how he had hit the big American man on the arm over and over. So I sneaked over to him. I meant no harm, but my intention was to scare the heck out of him. I came up behind him and did my rather poor imitation of a Godzilla growl, and the boy jumped five feet into the air. Mission accomplished. The young boy got the last laugh, though, because just as I was boarding the bus, I had a piece of corn on the cob hit me smack in the chest. The young boy was standing to the side smiling. Game over!

Once the village tour was over, it was followed by a visit to the porcelain boutique. The small boutique was rather hidden, and with so many other porcelain shops around, it made me wonder if there weren't some kickbacks in place. I was rather suspicious by this point and was not taking anything at face value. I am not a fan of porcelain, and the thought of trying to get it home without breaking it was more unwanted pressure, so while the families were in the boutique, I strolled the market area.

Just next door to the porcelain boutique was a jade shop, and in front of the jade shop was an independent vendor. I wasn't sure what he was selling, but a small crowd had gathered around him. I got as close as I could to see what could possibly be so interesting, and that's when I saw the snakes. There are only two kinds of snakes I fear; little ones and big ones. The vendor had several in a large white bag—I know this because an empty bag does not move around like that—but he also had several snakes on the ground in front of him. I had no idea what kind of snakes they were, and if they were poisonous or not, but I had gone as close as I was going to get.

The street was full of pedestrians, motorcycles, scooters, handcarts, and automobiles, all weaving in and out through the small cobblestone streets, barely avoiding a collision here or there. The traffic is so bad, Elaine told us a joke about a bus driver and a Chinese priest who both died and were met at the gate by St. Peter. When they were asked what they did for a living, the priest proclaimed his holiness and demanded to go in, but St. Peter refused the priest entry and allowed the bus driver to pass into heaven. The priest was furious and wanted an explanation. St. Peter told the priest that although he was a great speaker and made people listen to the word of God, the bus driver made his passengers call out, "Oh my God!" every day. I told you there would be more stories like this during our trip!

Kate also took the opportunity on the bus ride back to the hotel to talk about the Chinese diet and how important food is to them. Sitting down to a meal is an event, and many different types of foods are served. She said that yes, Chinese people eat a lot, but that because their food is low in sugar and they don't eat a lot of bread, they don't have the weight problems Americans have. Gee, thanks, I thought. I remembered a conversation my wife had had with Julia after one of our home studies. If the China program was really slowing down, Lorraine said, then why had China just signed an agreement with Italy to open the adoption program there? Julia told us that the Chinese would prefer that their babies go to Europeans because their perception of Americans is that we are all fat and unhealthy.

Kate wasn't my favorite person at the moment, and as I stepped off the bus in front of our hotel and walked past her, I found myself sucking in my gut. However, her next comment redeemed her just a little. Tara and her parents exited the bus right behind me, carrying Tara and their newest daughter. As they passed Kate, she reached out to them and said, "Thank you for what you are doing for these girls." Tara's mother stopped in her tracks and replied, "No, thank you for allowing us the opportunity to be parents to these precious little girls. We will be forever grateful to the Chinese government for allowing us the privilege of adopting our daughters." Wow, I thought, I could not have said it better myself. For all of my cynicism over this program, I have absolutely no complaints about the outcome. It truly is a privilege to have this child in our lives.

As Lorraine and I were riding the elevator up to our room, a couple from Spain was looking at Samantha and looking at me, then at Samantha again. The wife turned to her husband and in Spanish, remarked that the baby looked like her daddy. Imagine their surprise when I responded in Spanish, "That's what everyone is saying." It's easy to see how people mistake me for a Filipino and not Mexican-American. I wait for moments like that, and when they do happen, they rarely disappoint.

That afternoon, I went back to Tiffany's to pick up Samantha's loot. The woman who owned the shop had also taken it upon herself to get me a copy of Samantha's finding ad. When a baby is found abandoned, this is the ad that is run in the local paper with a picture to see if any family members will claim the baby. After the ad is run for a certain time, the baby is officially considered abandoned and processed in the system as such. It was the saddest thing I've ever seen. It broke my heart to see this newspaper page full of abandoned babies from that one day, with my sweet girl right in the middle of them all. I felt a weight on my heart as I walked back to the hotel.

While I was at Tiffany's, Lorraine had gone to Elaine's room to pick up a packet of three different documents that we would need to complete the paperwork for our adoption. One of them was Samantha's birth certificate, one was our adoption certificate, and one of them was a Certificate of Abandonment. Lorraine eyes welled up with tears as she told me, "It's the saddest thing I've ever seen. It just certifies that a search was made for her family and no one came forward to claim her."

Of course, we knew our child had been abandoned since that's the only way we were able to adopt her. However, having that vague notion and then seeing the actual evidence in black and white are two different things. It was a reality check, and it broke our hearts.

Lorraine and Samantha at The Glory Hotel

CHAPTER NINETEEN

THAT THURSDAY NIGHT, WE ALL met for our final dinner in Nanchang. Geoff and Melody did not join us because it seemed "Confucius's revenge" had hit Geoff. We took a short walk to a local restaurant. The lazy Susan was a recurring theme, and Lorraine and I ventured to try almost everything that circled our way. Samantha was content sitting in her high chair looking around and crinkling some paper.

After dinner, a few of us went and hung out in the hotel lounge for the last time. The lounge at Nanchang was a great refuge for us displaced Americans. Lorraine and I had spent a good bit of our free time in the lounge with other members of the group just to talk and reflect on our experiences in China and swap stories about our new babies. It really was our home away from home. Families in our group would wander in and out during the day, some would wave on their way out, and others would stop and chat on their way in. Several of the families were regulars; others were just cordial visitors.

The lounge was also a hangout for the rest of the guests in the hotel, including the European families that were there adopting babies. It was strange watching them hold their babies in one arm and wave a cigarette in the other. They seemed less concerned about the ill effects of smoking than we are in America. It was not our country, and we had no say in the making of the rules, but it was definitely not a sight you see much in our part of the woods.

The camaraderie of our group relieved the stress of being in a strange land. It made the five days we had to stay in Nanchang much easier to bear. We were all Americans, and it felt good to have that aspect of home right there with us as we were stuck right in the middle of the People's Republic of China. I look back and think of our many rendezvous at the lounge as one of the few highlights of Nanchang.

Even though we didn't spend as much time with some families in our travel group, we all kept up with the well-being of each other's babies. The couple we had flown with from Japan had a scary evening with their daughter one night when she became listless and unresponsive. Our leaders immediately recognized that the baby was dehydrated and took action. They took this couple and their baby to an emergency room. Granted, this was the middle of the night, but it turned out that that particular emergency room was closed, so they had to find another one. The next one they went to wasn't fully equipped to help, but they did put an IV in the baby to help her regain some fluid. Then, it was on to the next emergency room, dragging around the IV attached to the baby.

Needless to say, the experience was a nightmare for this couple. Fortunately, the baby got the care she needed, her appetite returned, and she was just fine. All of the families were genuinely concerned for this baby, and we did our best to keep each other informed.

As much as we enjoyed our hangout at the Glory Hotel, generally everyone just wanted to get out of Nanchang and get to our final destinations. I think there was an uneasiness with still being in the area where the children's birth mothers and families were. It was like we could be walking down the street and hear, "Stop, that's my baby." No one ever spoke out about it, but I think we all felt that undercurrent of fear, especially when we were all being gawked at so openly by the locals. Even the maid who took care of our room seemed to study all the babies very closely, as if she were looking for some family resemblance. It sounds crazy, but the more I think about it, the more I don't see why that couldn't happen. Then again, we were probably just paranoid.

There were actually two families in our group that had adopted before in China. One of the families had brought their daughter Tara along, and the other family had chosen to leave their young toddler at home. Others in the group often looked to these couples for advice, as they were more knowledgeable of the in and outs of the system. The family that didn't bring their daughter had actually been in Nanchang before for their first adoption. I noticed that they frequently went out on excursions by themselves. It was much later, in fact, after we had returned home, that we discovered they had gone to visit one of the foster homes in the area to see if they could get more information on their first daughter's background. Unfortunately, they had to be very secretive to protect all the parties involved.

Another member of our group was secretly trying to plan a trip to a local orphanage and was trying to get everyone to go. Lorraine and I didn't really want to see firsthand the place where our daughter was NOT taken care of, plus we did not want to rock the boat. Eventually, our leaders found out about the plan and put the kibosh on it. It just wasn't going to happen. The secrecy and discretion of the Chinese adoption program had the final word on that little excursion.

On that last night, Samantha woke up just a few times, and in the morning she was all smiles and blessed us with her happy babbling. We busied ourselves with packing and getting ourselves ready for the next leg of our journey.

There were only a few hours left before we headed to Nanchang International Airport to catch the last in-country flight to Guangzhou. It would be our last stop, and by then, I was ready to get home. Samantha had done well for about three days, but her nose was really starting to get runny again, and the gurgling when she breathed was more pronounced. The antibiotics that we had given her helped a little, but it was clear that Samantha was much sicker than we had realized. Guangzhou was where we would get the medical examination for Samantha, finish the adoption process, and take her home! Even though it was the last leg of our trip, we still had to stay for five more days.

We were being summoned to the hotel lobby for boarding on the bus that would take us to the airport. I didn't know what to expect in Guangzhou, but it couldn't be anything more unusual than Nanchang!

CHAPTER TWENTY

SAMANTHA WAS DOING AS WELL as could be expected, and she was definitely a trouper. My heart went out to her as she struggled to breathe. I was very concerned, yet I was fascinated with her ability to overlook how she felt and just focus on Lorraine and me.

I think Lorraine and I were just happy to be leaving Nanchang, mainly because we were scheduled to see the adoption physician in Guangzhou when we arrived on Saturday. This was a regimented stop on our schedule, a requirement needed to complete the adoption, and I must say Lorraine and I were more than a little worried. Most babies had colds and congestion, but Samantha's ongoing sickness was by far the most serious case of them all, and we were soon to find out just how serious.

Journal entry five

Last Day in Nanchang
Date: 06/28/2007

We leave today on the last leg of our trip, the city of Guangzhou. It has been an interesting trip to say the least. We have seen many things here in Nanchang that opened our eyes to the critical situation here in China. It only made us appreciate the reason we are here. Samantha is improving every day. She is still a little congested, but is such a happy baby. She smiles first thing in the morning when she sees us and reaches out to us to touch and make sure we're near. She is definitely in control here. We go now to the U.S. Consulate in Guangzhou and then we can come home. Hugs and kisses to all the family and we can't wait till we can present to all our little bundle of joy. Talk again soon.

Love to all,

Carlos, Lorraine, and Samantha Pineda

"The Lounge" Nanchang, Jiangxi

CHAPTER TWENTY-ONE

ON THE BUS RIDE TO the airport, our leaders handed out our daughters' new Chinese passports, bringing us one step closer to completing what needed to be done before we could leave the country and get our babies home. Leaving Nanchang's International Airport was fairly quick and easy. The volume of people traveling was fair but not large in comparison to, say, Atlanta-Hartsfield or Dallas–Fort Worth Airport in the States. In comparison, when we arrived in Guangzhou's International Airport, it was as if we had entered a scene from Stephen King's The Langoliers. We arrived late on a Friday night, and the airport was like a ghost town. It gave Lorraine and me the creeps. We traveled down the empty corridors and entered an isolated lobby headed toward the baggage claim, wondering where all the people had gone. The baggage claim showed more signs of life, but the corridors still echoed as our group moved through them.

On the bus ride to the hotel, we were joined by another Children's Hope operative named Tom. Tom was the only male representative we had during our stay in China, and during the following week, he would give us some new and interesting perspectives. During the ride, Tom told us a little about Guangzhou and explained that it was a big city like New York. I admit I was a little skeptical when he said this, but as the city came into view, his description was certainly apt. The city was lighted up, and there were many large buildings and skyscrapers. He also recommended that we try a Chinese beer called Green River during our stay. It was really quite good and very light, and it became my beer of choice for the rest of our visit in Guangzhou.

We finally arrived at the White Swan Hotel and waited our turn to check in. In front of us was a group of very smartly dressed people from one of the airlines—European pilots and flight attendants. During our stay, we saw airline personnel from all over the world, some of whose uniforms more closely resembled costumes, as they were suited in their native garb.

The White Swan is a five-star hotel and it was absolutely gorgeous! We had read that it was going to be under renovation during our visit and that we would have to stay at another hotel, but we were lucky and the renovations had not been started.

The White Swan, like the Glory Hotel, was where adopting families stayed during their last week in China. When my wife grumbled that she didn't understand why we couldn't stay at a cheaper hotel, I reminded her that it was part of the show. The Chinese government wanted your last impression of China to be the stunning waterfalls, botanical gardens, and artwork contained within the White Swan.

We spent several minutes at the front desk waiting to check in, and everyone, once they had their key, went to their rooms to wait for the luggage, which was, again, fifteen to twenty minutes behind us. The rooms were nice and the crib was really a baby crib. I felt better about Samantha sleeping in this crib compared with the wooden pallet bed in Nanchang. It was a bigger room than we had had in Nanchang, with a sitting and kitchen area by a very large window that looked out onto the river and the city.

We sat Samantha on one of the beds propped up with pillows and surrounded by her toys while we unpacked. I had to take a moment to just stop and look at her. She was smiling and babbling and had started reaching for and playing with her toys. I felt such joy at her transformation in such a short time with us, and yet was not without a certain sense of melancholy. As I watched this precious little girl, it was bittersweet knowing we were taking her from her birthplace, her culture, her heritage, and her past. I cried inside for her, and I just had to go and hold her for a moment before we resumed unpacking. I could only hope that Lorraine and I would be able to instill in her a sense of pride for her cultural heritage and, more than anything, the knowledge that her abandonment and the poor care she received were not her fault. The most important thing to me is for her to know that none of this was her fault.

Our settling in was interrupted by a knock on the door: the "turn-down" service. I'd never stayed in a hotel this fancy before and was both amused and irritated. I was amused that someone would even need this service and irritated that it meant another tip and more money out of my pocket. We declined this service for the rest of our stay but were sure to get the chocolates that came with it.

The room had two full-sized beds, so Lorraine and I knew we would be sleeping well. I was so glad to be able to stretch out. Since Nanchang's twin bed adventure, neither Lorraine nor I had slept very well. Finally, that night I was going to sleep next to my wife on a bed that we fit together on, and hold her tight while we drifted off for a full night's sleep. Not! Samantha hated the crib. She was so used to sleeping on the bed from our stay in Nanchang that we had to make up the second bed for her if we wanted to get any sleep. The only saving grace was that at least now, Lorraine and I had a tad bit more room on the full-size bed than the twin bed in Nanchang.

The hotels in China all provided two to three complimentary bottles of fresh water because the tap water was not safe to drink. We were warned not to drink the tap water or even use it to brush our teeth. We were instructed to put a wash towel over the faucet to remind us not to drink the water. In Beijing, I actually turned the faucet on and filled a glass about halfway; it was disgusting. I later found out that the toothpaste that was also complimentary was later involved in a recall because of the high levels of ethylene glycol, a base used in automobile antifreeze. The water in fact was dangerous, and several times both Lorraine and I forgot and caught ourselves trying to rinse our mouths out after brushing our teeth. I didn't quite remember in time while in Nanchang and spent eight to ten hours with Confucius's revenge! I made the same mistake in Guangzhou by ordering up a glass with ice for my drink, because I wanted to drink something cold. It, too, caused me grief.

Lorraine and I would venture down every morning to have breakfast in the hotel dining room, and each time we would meet many Americans who were all in China for different reasons. Like

Lorraine and me, some were there for the adoption process. Some were there on vacation, and some were there for business purposes. We also ran into two families that were there on a ten-year reunion tour. The family's children were eleven and twelve years old. I remember talking to Lorraine about the possibility of a trip in ten years, but at the time she wasn't very receptive. I know that as time goes on, she will want the best for Samantha, and we will certainly leave this option open to her.

CHAPTER TWENTY-TWO

IT WAS SATURDAY IN GUANGZHOU, and it was medical examination day. Lorraine and I had stayed up most of the night talking about what we would do, and we both agreed we would be brutally honest regardless of what happened. Understand, this was a hard decision for us since we had no idea what the CCAA would do and how they would react to what we were going to tell them. Samantha was sick and needed medicine. We were afraid they might take Samantha back and offer us a "healthy baby" or detain us from leaving because of the bureaucracy, and we would get "the treatment." I have no idea what that means, but it sounded evil. Anyway our concerns were legitimate, and we were scared.

Eventually it was time to gather at the front of our hotel for our medical exam. We actually walked to the Medical Examination Center from the hotel, but we had to stop and have a picture made in a little Chinese convenience store for a document needed at the American Consulate. The walk to the medical center was about twenty minutes through the quaint streets surrounding the hotel. It was a pretty picture, sort of like a neighborhood stroll through Mayberry but much more colorful.

We passed many small shops along the way, and the local shop owners hustling in front of the shops did their best to make us veer off course and into their shops. We would visit them later, but we had much more important business to deal with at that moment! The closer we got to the medical center, the more dread we felt. We knew it was important to Samantha's health and that kept us on the straight and narrow, but we also were afraid of the reaction we might receive. Many things went through our heads as we walked in silence holding each other's hand.

The medical center was full of Chinese children with different ailments waiting to see the physician or waiting for prescription medicine. The adoption clinic was around the side of the main entrance, and there was another group, one of the adoption groups that we were with in Nanchang, right before us. They were just wrapping up, and we were next in line. The clinic was clean, with two small, private examination spots on opposite sides of the room. We were given forms to fill out in regard to the health of our babies. The questions were tricky, and I wasn't sure how to answer, so I scratched through them and just wrote down Samantha's symptoms.

You could hear the babies crying as we all took turns waiting to see the examiner. There were nurses weighing the children, and then another nurse would measure the children while yet another nurse recorded all of the information.

The time had come for Lorraine and me to take Samantha into the examination room. The physician in charge was an older Chinese lady who was stoic and spoke very little English. She quickly began her examination and after reading our form began asking us questions. We described Samantha's symptoms as she put the stethoscope to Samantha's chest and looked into her ears. Unfortunately by this time, we felt it was strictly for show. The doctor then in broken English told us, "Go get your leader." Lorraine was in tears. It was evident that there was a sense of urgency in the examination room and that all the buzz was about Samantha. This was a sick little girl and the doctor knew it!

We told the doctor we had given Samantha a round of antibiotics that we'd brought with us from America. She shook her head and said, "American medicine no good."

We were told to move to the next station while Elaine was talking to the doctor about Samantha. As primitive as we may have thought most of the examination would be, we hadn't expected a squeaky toy as part of the hearing test. However, the next nurse used a small rubber-duck squeaky toy to test Samantha's hearing. Samantha, being

Samantha, was too busy studying the nurse to pay attention and didn't even respond to the squeaky toy. I don't know what the point of the test was since she checked that Samantha's hearing was fine anyway.

We were then quickly escorted to another room, where we had to wait for another doctor, who gave us a prescription for an antibiotic and medicine for her congestion. Turned out, Samantha had bronchitis and a double ear infection. I was very worried because Samantha had been ill when we'd received her in Nanchang, and that had been nearly a week before. My concern was for any possible damage to her hearing since that much time had passed without medical treatment. The only thing that might have helped was the antibiotics we'd received before we made the trip to China. My stomach was in knots, and I worried for Lorraine, who by this time was an emotional wreck. The talk around us was about Samantha, but it was being spoken in Chinese, and we had no idea what was going on.

Journal entry six

Medical Exam

Date: 06/30/2007

I want to say first and foremost that Samantha is doing much better, although it was found in her exam that she has bronchitis, a double ear infection, and swollen tonsils due to the congestion she had when we got her Sunday. It's hard to believe it since she is such a happy child. We were asked to fill out a questionnaire that had very vague questions and we found it hard to put correct answers that fit the current situation. We had talked to each other about this situation prior and were committed to doing all that was necessary to get Samantha the medical treatment she so desperately needed. I scratched out the original questions and put our concerns in handwriting underneath the original questions. This did not bode well with the Chinese doctors, and the reaction was such that it scared Lorraine and brought her to tears, thinking there might be a possibility they may keep Samantha in China longer. That didn't turn out to be the case, thank God! They gave us some medicine to loosen the phlegm and antibiotics for her ear and tonsil infection. Again I say she is fine so please don't worry.

Lorraine was more upset at the fact they gave her to us very congested and she worried about the treatment and care they gave her before we came to the rescue. This morning Samantha was her usual happy self. We will have our Pedi check her when we get home, and believe us when we say home is where we want to be!

Medical Examination Room in Guangzhou

CHAPTER TWENTY-THREE

THE REST OF THE GROUP had finished up and went back to the hotel, whereas Lorraine and I had to wait for the final exam and prescription drugs. We finally received the medicine and were told we could leave. We found out later that the antibiotics prescribed for Samantha were discontinued in America because of the awful taste. I just wanted to get her home. I had never in my life felt so helpless, and what made this situation worse was that I had no confidence in the medical staff that was attending to Samantha. God help us!

When we returned to the White Swan Hotel, it was warming to know that there were families waiting with concern for Samantha's health. Lorraine and I never hid the fact that we were concerned that Samantha was very ill, even though at times Samantha didn't act like she was ailing. Samantha was a tough little girl, and that attitude would help Lorraine and I get through the next few months.

The next few days in China were critical, and it was going to be important that we stay on schedule with the medication. Samantha was not taking to this medicine very well because of the awful taste, and she had to have four ounces at a time! We modified it somewhat by mixing it with fruit juice so Samantha would drink it, but the taste was so bad it was still a challenge. It would provide enough of a relief for Samantha to make the journey home. We were really grateful for the prayer support as well as the moral support from all the families. Lorraine probably appreciated that a tad bit more because of her emotional condition through all this. Mind you, Lorraine is no wimp. I've always considered her my rock, but this involved Samantha and it may have been too much. I felt so bad for both my girls.

The one thing that I had reservations about during and after the medical exam was that neither Lorraine nor I, and as a matter of fact, none of the families, would be allowed to see the final medical data written in the child's information file. The files were the property of the government and strictly confidential. This confidential report might have helped us, because the report that we had received with Samantha's initial papers came back to haunt us when we returned to the States. We had the medical records translated by our pediatrician back home. He solemnly called us into his office to explain to us that these records contained information on a young male child who was mentally challenged, HIV positive, and HEP B positive, and had a badly deformed clubfoot. Pretty exaggerated description for a little girl with a serious flu virus! However, his birth date was the same as Samantha's and his name was also "Wang Qui something." Getting the incorrect paperwork or medical records was definitely one of our worst fears. We ended up redoing all of her immunizations and testing when we got home, but I think we would have done it anyway. We had been told that the vaccinations they gave the babies and children in China were ones they received from other countries after the medicine had expired.

While Lorraine and Samantha took a nap in the room, I ventured downstairs for a quick smoke. As I got off the elevators to return to our room, I ran into Tara's mother, who quickly asked me how we were all doing. I said, "I just want to get her home so she can see our doctor." She smiled at me warmly and knowingly as she replied, "That's exactly what my husband said when we were in China to get Tara. She had pneumonia and we were scared the whole time we were here." It was nice talking to someone who truly knew where I was coming from.

I went back to the room to check on my girls. They were awake, and Lorraine was packing up the diaper bag for our afternoon excursion with our group to a trade mall. On the way there, Tom gave us the layout of the mall and told us where to get the highest-quality pearls and where the stores were. He also gave us a lesson on bartering, such as looking at the price, taking off a certain percentage, and offering that price. He was very specific, and that advice was much more helpful than a general "Go forth and barter." The mall was huge. It was seven or eight stories high, and there were four buildings surrounding a plaza that contained the food court.

We had planned on buying jade and pearls, or actually I had planned on buying jade, but my wife for some reason would not allow me to buy any jade. Puzzled, I asked why. Apparently Lorraine's mother had told her that jade was bad luck! I protested, but she begged me not to buy it and I finally gave in. It wasn't until we got back to the States that we found out Lorraine was mistaken. My mother-in-law had actually said jade was good luck, but of course, it was too late. I was fortunate enough to buy some pearl items. I bought Lorraine a beautiful double necklace of pearls that she would be able to pass down to Samantha when she was older. I was able to get our mothers and our house sitters pearls as well. I still regret not being able to take advantage of the jade market. Bad luck—*please!*

There were of course many different shops in the mall besides jewelry shops, and I found one store that carried pirated DVDs and CDs. I am a huge fan of the Marvel Comics superheroes, so I follow movies based on them very closely. This was June 2007, and although *The Fantastic Four—Rise of the Silver Surfer* movie was scheduled for release in late June in the United States, it was already available for sale at this particular store. What I found odd was that the DVD packaging actually said it was filmed with a camcorder and listed which DVD players were compatible. There were many counterfeit items available in this mall. The Chinese called them knock-offs. Resourceful, aren't they?

That evening, several other couples invited us to dine with them at a restaurant called Lucy's Place. It replaced the lounge in Nanchang and became a regular hangout for several of the families. It didn't have the relaxing setting like the lounge in Nanchang, but it was air-conditioned, and it had the coldest beer in Guangzhou. That was good enough for me. It was more the social gathering that drew us together—the beer was a near second, but the togetherness was the most important. At times, being in China had the feel of "us and them," as it would anytime you're in a strange environment.

Lucy's had wall-to-wall Americanized decor. There were posters of Charlie Chaplin and James Dean, and license plates from various states and cities in America. They sold Budweiser and Miller Lite beer. Their menu had fried chicken, hot dogs, hamburgers, onion rings, and French fries. It was the closest we were going to get to American cuisine, and we sopped it up—although, again, that egg appeared in the strangest places. Just like the lounge in Nanchang, it was the camaraderie between families that made Lucy's the place to be!

Lorraine and Samantha at Lucy's

Chapter Twenty-four

On Sunday morning, I stayed with Samantha while Lorraine went to a conference room so our representatives could help everyone fill out the paperwork for the consulate.

I waited for Lorraine to return so I could continue my usual morning ritual of venturing out, first to the business center to update my Web page for the families back home, and then for a regular stroll with my coffee and cigarette. In Nanchang, I became close friends with the bellboys and doorman mainly because there was not much scenery around the Glory Hotel, but in Guangzhou it was very different. The area was surrounded by small, modest shops, the streets were lined with tall, full trees, and the sidewalks were paved in different-sized stones—just a picturesque view, pleasant to the eyes and safe for strolling, unlike the surroundings in Nanchang. Guangzhou truly was an international city, and the people there had a completely different attitude from those in Nanchang and even in Beijing. I met several of the shopkeepers during my morning strolls. They introduced themselves with their Americanized names like Betty, Julie, and my favorite, Coco.

They became part of our daily routine. I would drop off the laundry at Coco's little shop, and she even gave us a free stroller to use during our stay. It gave me a feeling of comfort as Lorraine, Samantha, and I would pass these shops during the day and the shop owners would greet us by name. I know it was more of a sales gimmick—and it worked because we did have a tendency to visit and spend money in their shops—but it was still a nice feeling.

Lorraine and I did spend some money; maybe it was our way of keeping our minds occupied. It must have worked because we kept spending and spending money. I must admit I was starting to feel like a tourist and was having fun. Samantha's well-being was always our first priority, but I would be lying if I told you I wasn't glad for the distraction.

Later that afternoon, as I was returning to our hotel room after a laundry drop, the staff at the White Swan stopped me and handed me a complimentary Barbie doll. This wasn't your typical Barbie, but an Adoption Barbie carrying a small Chinese baby—a blonde, blue-eyed Barbie dressed in typical Barbie fashion with a miniskirt and high heels. This made me uncomfortable, and I really had to think about what bothered me so much about it. I finally realized that the Chinese seemed just too comfortable with the whole adoption process and giving away their babies. The blatant disconnect from the many female infants leaving the country was unsettling! To me, that Barbie represented how adoption had become more of a commercialized venture than the emotional event it truly was.

I brought the Barbie up to our room to show Lorraine. She took one look at it and said, "How bizarre! I guess I'll tuck it away as a novelty piece for when Samantha gets older." On that note, we gathered Samantha and left the hotel for a family outing.

During our excursions in Guangzhou, we found a local merchant who told us her name was Judy, and she worked in a shop owned by her brother called Jordan's. We would spend a large portion of our income in her gift shop because she really worked with us on the prices and was extremely pleasant to do business with. It was the street vendors who absolutely epitomized the capitalist attitude of up-sell, up-sell, up-sell. I can still hear them saying, "Oh, you need this, too. It say, 'I love you, baby.'" Judy was quiet and sweet and made the experience normal, and I really appreciated it, but it was still fun to listen to the vendors and their hard-sell tactics. I had actually bought a knock-off Rolex that looked real—real enough for an airline employee to take it from my luggage before it arrived home. I paid only $8 for it, so the loss wasn't great, but it did look real and would have made a great conversation piece. Oh well, easy come, easy go!

There were all kinds of activities around our hotel, from all the vendors to the exercise classes that we observed on the lawn area adjacent to the hotel. There were also some very interesting bronze life-sized statues on the street. One was a set of three women that we thought was kind of cool. The first was in traditional garb, the next was in a business suit, and the next was a young woman with short shorts and high heels, with a cell phone up to her ear. Apparently, this was a depiction of the evolution of women in China. There was another statue nearby of a very large woman in a sundress walking a pug. Lorraine and I looked at each other and she asked, "Do you think that's their depiction of an American tourist?" I think that's exactly what it was.

The White Swan truly is a beautiful hotel. It has large waterfalls and is landscaped wonderfully with Delilah, Lemon Button, and purple waffle ferns, and royal poinciana, ylang-ylang, and other varieties of tropical trees. The large pond is full of large, beautiful koi or more specifically, nishikigoi. They are believed to have originated from East Asia, Aral, and the Black and Caspian seas. The earliest records of koi have been found in China, and they have been widely spread in Korea and Japan.

The artistry and décor of the hotel are unique in fashion. The shops are upscale and quite expensive, but like the rest of the vendors in China, there is a haggling system, and if you know how to do it, it will save you a lot of money.

I am a smoker—mostly of cigarettes, but I have been known to dabble in cigars. I love a good Cuban cigar! As everyone is well aware, it is illegal to purchase Cuban cigars in the United States. That rule did not apply to China. I was caught frequently enjoying a Cuban cigar, and I loved every minute of it! I am guilty of actually bringing a few home—but enough about my personal vices.

While we were in China, Hong Kong was celebrating the tenth anniversary of its independence from England. In Guangzhou, we would get a newspaper every morning in English, so we saved several of papers with the celebratory headlines. It was pretty cool that we were there for such a historical milestone.

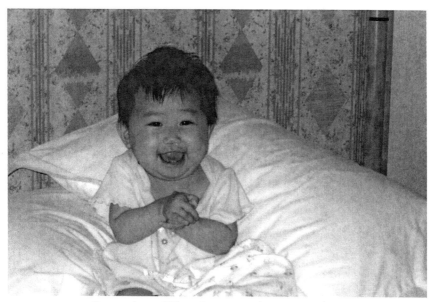

Samantha at White Swan Hotel in Guangzhou

CHAPTER TWENTY-FIVE

THE NEXT FEW DAYS FOR Samantha were good ones. She seemed to be responding to the medication—at least she appeared to be getting healthier. Her breathing was still a little gurgly, but it was better, and the flow of stringy yellow mucus had slowed down some, although we were still cautious. It was hard to believe Samantha was so ill, especially since she was such a happy baby. The change in her personality was evident. In just eight days, she made us feel like she was comfortable with her strange caregivers. She was also responding to her new name, Samantha. It was so much fun frolicking around with her in the room, on the floor, and on the bed. Her laugh was medicine for Lorraine and me. We were filled with a false sense of security that she might be back to good health. She was a gorgeous and resilient little girl, and how we loved her!

On September 6, 1996, I was involved in an accident at work that caused me to lose three fingers on my left hand; my index, middle finger, and ring finger were removed. I mention this only because I spent many years hiding my hand in shame and embarrassment. I found most people to be shocked by the sight of my missing fingers, but the one constant was the lack of reaction from children. I have six grandchildren, and none of them have a problem with Grandpa's hand. They would touch it and ask what happened, and I would tell them Grandma bit my fingers off, but to them, it was still Grandpa's hand. Samantha didn't seem to mind either. She would hold my pinky finger and rub the knobs of the remaining fingers and not bat an eyelash. It was important to me, since I don't think I truly have gotten comfortable with the appearance of my left hand. To Samantha, missing fingers and all, I was Dad! This meant the world to me!

Journal entry seven

All Is Well with Samantha

Date: 07/01/2007

The medication that they gave us to give her seemed to have helped a little. She seems to have a little bounce to her and is giving us all she has and it is a lot! It is amazing to us when we realize that just one week ago today we picked up this scared, distrusting (with every reason), sick and screaming little child. Today she is just a happy, normal, and wonderful gift of love. We could not have dreamed a happier, more perfect ending to this journey in our wildest moment. We are truly blessed. Two more days here and we can go home. We are ready. Carlos, Lorraine, and Samantha

Carlos, Lorraine, Geoff and Melody babies

99

CHAPTER TWENTY-SIX

ON MONDAY MORNING, WE WERE instructed to stay in our rooms again as our leaders were putting together the final papers for the consulate so we would be available if any questions arose. We had to wait until noon, and as soon as our time was up, we left the hotel for a stroll and a quick lunch at Lucy's before returning to our room to get ready for yet another appointment.

A tradition in the adoption community featured a group photograph of the newly adopted children on a red couch. I had read somewhere that the first group of children adopted from China had posed on the red couch in the lobby area of the White Swan. Therefore, it became customary for each new group of adopted babies to have a group shot on that same red couch. Easier said than done! I let my wife take the reins on this project. She told me she had an adorable outfit for Samantha to wear, another generous gift from one of her coworkers, and I have to say it was pretty cute. All the babies looked adorable, some of them dressed in their traditional Chinese dresses made at Tiffany's.

Imagine trying to get fifteen babies, some of whom struggled to sit up on their own, to pose for a picture on a red couch in the center of a busy lobby surrounded by all the families. Now there's a challenge. In the end, I took several pictures myself, and not once could I get Samantha to look forward. I knew which one was her in the picture, though, since I knew where she was positioned in the group, but also because her profile exaggerated her thin head, and she was very recognizable. She was more interested in feeling the silky dress of the baby beside her than in posing for a picture.

I got pictures of the mothers trying to hide behind the couch while holding their babies. I got several where half of the children were looking the opposite way, and by the time I took the last picture, there was just a lot of crying going on. The scene was quite entertaining.

Lorraine and I were able to participate in several of the extra group activities now that we felt Samantha was doing so well, at least well enough to let us participate in them. During our stay in Nanchang, we had bowed out of some of the group dinners and a little birthday party they threw for one of the babies.

We signed up for an optional dinner cruise that evening. On the bus ride there, Tom warned us that dinner would be served buffet-style and to not be surprised if the locals just hopped in front of us. Unlike Americans, the Chinese rarely form lines to do anything. The term "gang-rushed" had a whole new meaning in China. When the bell rang, I thought of the famous words of the Kentucky Derby: "And they're off!"

The cruise took us down the Pearl River, where we enjoyed the lights of the city from both banks. The city skyline was elegant. Lights outlined the larger buildings, and some of the buildings' exteriors had flashing designs of various patterns and swirls. The scenery along the banks was spectacular, and we were fortunate that evening to actually watch a storm in the distance with a tremendous lightning show. The dinner was different. Unfortunately, I had not gotten used to the Chinese cuisine. I had tried many new items and Cantonese cuisine is definitely a must in Guangzhou, but nine days into the trip, my sense of adventure about food had rapidly declined. Eating blue, shaped balls, dry, cold, and sloppy noodles, and the mystery meat (eel, squid, turtle, etc.) was a challenge I grew weary of!

We sat and had dinner with the couple who had adopted a special-needs child. Their daughter had a cleft lip and palate, although her lip was already repaired and looked just perfect. She was a little older, too, I think around sixteen months. The couple told us that their daughter had been in a foster home and had gotten really good care, which explained why this little girl did not seem behind developmentally at all. The unfortunate thing was that she was supposed to have spent that last week before this couple came to get her in the local orphanage to try to give her a transition period. Instead, they had to pick her up straight from her foster family, and it was very traumatic. So far, the little girl had bonded only with her new dad and wanted nothing to do with her new mom. We offered them assurances that it would change and everything would work out—something they knew, of course, but it didn't keep the wife from looking pretty uncertain and unhappy about it at the time.

We really felt sorry for her as we watched her try to reach out to her new daughter several times only to be rebuffed at each attempt. I would love to know how they are doing now.

We were anxious about getting close to our final stop—the American Consulate. This is where we would take our oath to pledge to be responsible for our newly adopted daughter. You would think that would be the end of the process, but once we returned to the States, there would be three more home study reports, a readoption process, passport registration, obtaining a Social Security card, etc., so there was no fat lady singing yet! I must admit though, that the idea of going home was most appealing. I was ready.

There were several things in China that I wish I could duplicate here at home. The laundry service was definitely the first thing. I hope that doesn't sound too stereotypical, but damn, they were good. It was inexpensive, too. At home, Lorraine is responsible for the laundry, but in China, taking care of the laundry had become part of my daily routine. Every couple of days, I would swing by Coco's after my morning cigarette and drop off the family laundry and then swing by in the evening to pick it up. In Guangzhou, there were many to choose from. I counted ten laundry businesses in a two-block radius of the hotel. However, I stayed loyal to Coco because her place did a great job and went out of their way to go the extra mile for me and my family.

During the course of our trip, families had sort of divided into little groups. Somebody had said they felt the groups divided into a social ranking status. You know: I-drive-a-Mercedes-and-you're-in-a-Ford type of thing. However, I felt it was more of a glee-club-versus-the-marching-band sort of thing. It was inevitable that certain families would feel more comfortable with each other—that's human nature. I had no preconceived notions one way or the other about any person or any one group. It is what it is, but you know, it was this eclectic flavor that made our travels unique. All walks of life were represented in our little group. There were corporate executives, bankers, salespeople, secretaries, computer gurus, doctors, staffing consultants, teachers, welders, automotive technicians, and housewives, all on the same mission. It was our own little melting pot in China. You gotta love it.

Skyline at night in Guangzhou

CHAPTER TWENTY-SEVEN

Journal entry eight

Last Day in China
Date: 07/02/2007

Today is our last day in China. We have a 2:45 P.M. appointment with the American Consulate to be sworn in as Samantha's official parents. This has been an adventure of a lifetime. Guangzhou is a beautiful city. We have seen many different sides of the Chinese culture, eaten their original cuisine, drunk some of the local beer, and spent a lot of our American money. I count my blessings every day. As soon as I see Samantha's smiling face and Lorraine holding her in her arms, I know that I am the luckiest man in the world. I have truly been blessed, and I thank God for looking out for us during this trip and am so ready to get home and share this little wonderful bundle of joy! We miss you all and we will see you soon.
Carlos, Lorraine, and Samantha Pineda

The schedule for our last day in China was hectic. Aside from running around capping off the last of the adoption process, we had to pack and get ready to go home. Our American Consulate visit was scheduled for that afternoon, and we had our last dinner as a group planned for that night. We would be saying good-bye to each of the families that had endured the China experience with Lorraine and me, and it would allow us to see all the children together for what might be the last time.

The bus arrived to take us to the American Consulate around 2 P.M., and we loaded up and headed toward downtown. This is when we got Tom's male perspective on the Chinese bureaucracy. His thoughts on China's one-child policy were interesting; I don't think he was in favor of it. He was married and talked about needing permission from the government about when he and his wife could have a child. If the quota for newborn babies had been met for that year, couples were told they had to wait until the next year to start a family. The government actually suggested that couples live apart until they were allowed to have a child!

Tom seemed to have a certain disdain in his voice as he described how the rules applied to the people of China. He was a nice guy, and his views were a bit more westernized. He said he had a daughter and was actually excited that when she grew up, she would really be able to pick and choose whom she married. I remember someone in our group had asked Tom during one of our paperwork meetings if the Chinese people were allowed to vote for their political leaders. Tom continued going through the papers and just answered, "Well, if there was a vote, no one told me about it."

The American Consulate building had very tight security, and we had to go through a maze of stations and floors before reaching the offices of the adoption facility. We noticed many of the same groups from other agencies that we'd seen in Nanchang and in Guangzhou at the Medical Examination Center there at the consulate's office complex. It was another "hurry up and wait" scenario. Our Children's Hope reps gathered the group and herded us to an empty batch of chairs and told us to sit and wait. Thirty minutes later they returned and formed us into several lines in front of teller-type windows and gave us final instruction as to what information and paperwork would be needed when we reached the window. After the window ordeal, we all took our seats again and waited several minutes until an older, heavyset American lady began to ask for everyone's attention.

The time to take the oath had arrived. It was simple and it was quick, but it was still meaningful to Lorraine and me. It was your basic "I promise to guard and protect …" type of oath. We were out in the street and back on the bus within minutes of completing the oath, and headed back to the hotel. We would meet again in an hour or so to have one last dinner together as a group.

We loaded the bus and headed off to some restaurant that Elaine, Gloria, and Tom had selected for the group. Elaine would tell stories and give info as we scooted from place to place on the bus, but today was special. We all knew this was the last time we would be assembled as a group and that we may never see some of these families again. I will definitely miss them. These people shared one of the most special times in our life. Even other people who have adopted in China and gone to the same province won't share the same memories that we will have with these fifteen families. Our experience was unique to this group, and no one else will ever know all that we experienced together.

Elaine gave us a little heartwarming speech, but it was Gloria who brought us all to tears, even yours truly—okay, especially yours truly. Gloria had been the quieter one throughout most of this trip. Sort of the Hardy to the Laurel, the Abbott to the Costello—you get the picture. We were chanting "Gloria, Gloria" to see if we could get her to say a few words. We got what we asked for.

Gloria started out well, saying how she was happy to be part of this group's journey and how everyone was so nice to her. Then came the killer part. It made it even more meaningful because she cried as she spoke, her voice shaky and tears streaming down her cheeks. She told us she was so grateful to see how we, the families, attended to our children first. Even when we were tired and hungry, she saw how we always put the babies first and how much we loved them. I don't remember the rest because I was so trying so hard to get my emotions under control. God, I hate trying to be macho! We finally arrived at the restaurant, and the dinner was enjoyable. Tom seemed to always be on hand to help us identify the foods going by us on the lazy Susan. We stayed at the restaurant for quite a while. As we finished eating, we all went back and forth, visiting with each other and taking a lot of pictures. The thought of going home began to surface as a reality, and I was glad. We had been in China fifteen days, and it was time to go home!

Last Dinner in Guangzhou with Geoff and Melody

CHAPTER TWENTY-EIGHT

I HAVE BEEN LOW-KEY ABOUT our faith in this writing because I wanted people to read our story and not be put off by any overbearing religious messages. However, Lorraine and I have no doubts that the things that happened were part of our destiny, and it was just fate the way things transpired. There were just too many coincidental events that took place that could be explained only by divine intervention. The gracious hand of God followed us, helped and guided us all throughout the process, and took care of Samantha while we were in China. This I know, and for that, I am eternally grateful.

My wife has said more than once that the hand of God is in that matching room at the CCAA. Every family thought they got the best baby because they got the perfect baby for them. Beyond even her looks, our child has the perfect personality for our family. She was just meant to be ours from the beginning, and we believe that with our whole hearts.

The next morning we checked out of the hotel around 4:30 A.M. Our Children's Hope representatives had the hotel box up our breakfast for us to take to the airport since we had to leave so early.

I thought the toughest part of our trip was over, but again, I was mistaken. During our time in Guangzhou, there had been a terrorist bombing at Glasgow International Airport on June 30, 2007. Even though we were distracted with our new child, this story was all over the news. We were able to find an English-speaking television station and followed this tragedy as much as we could. The world was on high security alert, which definitely affected our travels.

The security was extra tight at the airport in Guangzhou, and the lines were long as the airport personnel hand-searched all of our carry-on luggage. The flight out of Guangzhou was about four hours, and then, we had a brief layover in Tokyo. We had to get through two security checkpoints and thought that was tough, but the eleven-hour flight from Narita to Detroit, Michigan, was even more grueling.

Hindsight being 20/20, we would have, should have bought an extra seat for Samantha. We skimped on that expense and just kicked ourselves during that whole eleven-hour flight. It was a rough trip home. I have never experienced a flight so uncomfortable in my life. It was hard to eat because we could put only one tray down for Lorraine and me at a time. A young lady from Australia had the aisle seat on our row so we had to ask her to get up every time I had to go to the bathroom, every time Lorraine had to go, and every time Samantha had to be changed. Lorraine and I eventually quit drinking anything because we didn't want to have to bother that poor woman and because it was so hard climbing in and out of those coach seats. It would have definitely been to our advantage to buy the extra seat. I highly recommend it!

We might get some criticism for this, but we had packed some Benadryl. Because Samantha was crying a lot and was just as uncomfortable as we were, we gave her some, which knocked her out for a while. We had told some of the other families on our flight that we had it, and that bottle of Benadryl made the rounds.

Once we arrived in Detroit, our first port of call, we had to go through customs. There were several international planes that landed at almost the same time, and the giant room for customs was packed with very long lines. We thought the worst part was behind us, but going through customs nearly broke our spirits.

Be very careful when you disembark from the airplane that you ask specific questions of the airline hostess directing the lines as you enter the customs and immigration staging area. There is a particular line that is strictly for immigration and your new child's paperwork. We, of course, were not put in the right line, and as a result, missed our connecting flight to Atlanta.

If you end up in the wrong line, they will make you go to the correct line but to the end of it. It took Lorraine, Samantha, and I four and a half hours to get through customs and immigration. Samantha by this time had seen enough. Lorraine and I had run out of formula for her, and we were down to two diapers. We tried hard not to let our frustration out on each other, but once the panic of being out of formula and almost out of diapers hit us, we were just about at the end of our patience. These were the growing pains of being new and inexperienced parents.

We were very fortunate that the airline—and I tip my hat to them—was prepared and almost immediately rescheduled us on the next flight. The layover was really a blessing, but we had not realized it yet. It actually allowed us time to recompose ourselves. We were able to get a decent meal in us since during the flight home, we had given up on eating, too. It turned out that the last flight to Atlanta was almost empty, and we were able to use an extra seat for Samantha. This was a gift—a much-needed gift. Lorraine and I were tired, and we knew Samantha was tired, too. We had notified our family that we would be arriving two hours later than originally scheduled, and we were excited about having a group of friends and family waiting for us in Atlanta.

We were greeted in Atlanta with much fanfare by Lorraine's parents and Pam and Dar. We felt the tears coming all over again as we saw a big sign that read "Welcome home, Samantha."

As tired as we thought we were, we stayed up for quite a while once we got home to share our stories of China and bask in the glow of being home with our beautiful new daughter.

Journal entry nine

Back Home Safe and Sound
Date: 07/05/2007

Thank you all for viewing and sharing this wonderful time in our life. I will never be able to express in words the joy and pleasure of this wonderful journey of a lifetime. It has given Lorraine and me a new beginning with a beautiful and loving child. The bond between all of us is very strong.

Thank you all for being a part of it, and thanks to everyone for the support and the generosity shown to us as we start our lives as mentors and leaders in this young girl's life.

CHAPTER TWENTY-NINE

WE WERE SO GLAD TO be back at home, although we had no idea of the difficulties we would be facing. Samantha would have high fevers and seizures, and continue to battle with ear infections for the next few months. We would be in and out of the emergency room; we would change pediatricians several times while we battled to get Samantha the care she needed. It was all well worth it, though, because I am happy to report that Samantha is a very happy and healthy little girl.

We had been home for probably two months when we discovered that a foster mom in China was desperately looking for the adoptive parents of Wang, Qiu Fu. We are in several Internet groups that consist of families who are going or have been to China and have completed or are about to complete the adoption process. This is how news and information travels in the adoption community. Lorraine wasn't as prepared as I was for any transfer of information. The process was still too new, and the experience in China had left her very cautious. I, on the other hand, was more open to a line of communication, but strictly for Samantha. To appease Lorraine, I entered this situation slowly and always questioned whether she was comfortable with me continuing. I would not want to be the one getting these foster moms in trouble by giving too much information, but it turns out, they got in touch with a person who was here in America and this person finally contacted Lorraine and me via the group. After seeing the name of this contact person, I remembered the address label I had found on Samantha's foot. It was strange that I had kept it safe in my wallet, and when I pulled it out, it was a match!

Lorraine and I spent many nights discussing the possibility that Samantha may have been in foster care, but it was hard to believe since she was so ill and had been so behind developmentally. However, there were other signs that pointed to her being in foster care. Samantha had very high lead levels in her blood, whereas the other children from our adoption group had not experienced this problem. The foster mom in China had sent her American connection a letter with her address and a picture of Wang, Qiu Fu. Again, it was a match!

This really rocked our world. We had a decision to make and in that decision, we needed to consider Samantha first. We asked ourselves how far we were willing to go to keep a connection to her culture and heritage. It probably wouldn't have been such a calamity if the turmoil we'd gone through with Samantha being sick and the Chinese bureaucracy we'd had to endure hadn't been so fresh in our minds. This didn't make our decision any easier. There was still a bad taste in our mouths. It was difficult to hear how happy we should be that she was in a foster home and not an orphanage. It was difficult to believe that she was so loved when we had seen the shape she was in.

After much time and thought, Lorraine and I agreed to send a picture of Samantha to the foster mother, but we would not identify ourselves or give any information until we were ready. I have kept the letter for Samantha and will save it for her so when she's older; what she does with it will be in her hands. I felt it was our duty as the adoptive parents of a beautiful little girl from China to leave that communication and knowledge of these things for her consideration. We will send a picture every year until we feel it's time to let Samantha make that decision. It is our belief that this foster mother may even know Samantha's biological mother, so we want to keep that connection alive for Samantha's sake and her sake only. It is our duty.

Chapter Thirty

THERE ARE SO MANY STORIES to tell from our adventure, but I wanted to tell these particular stories for all the families out there enduring the same wait that we did. I wanted to share my layman's view of all that we witnessed in China. I wanted to share what we endured always wondering, Is it going to be my turn this month? The joys and the heartache and the uncertainty and the many questions you might have during the wait all tend to wear on the soul. Although we wanted to be happy for the families that received their referrals before us, we felt some shame that our well wishes were tinged with jealousy—the sadness of seeing a finished nursery and asking yourself, Will it ever happen for me? The Children's Hope agency sends out monthly updates faithfully, and when you know you are not in the next group, it does sting a little, but I always appreciated the information.

I tried to remain optimistic during our travels through China about the political situation and how that would drive the attitude. I never harbored ill feelings toward the Chinese people, because I know they do what they must to survive—it is a necessity. I felt that was the sentiment of the locals as we traveled through China.

I remember coming home from the military in 1978 after spending some time overseas and wanting to kiss the ground as I landed in the United States. This was the feeling I appreciated and carried with me for many years—knowing in my heart that America, to me, was the greatest place in the world. I returned home from China with that same feeling.

I enjoyed the sightseeing while in China, and our agency did a terrific job of walking the families through the process from city to city. The agency representatives were awesome, and I am so glad we chose to go through Children's Hope. I would definitely recommend them to anyone wanting to adopt from China or other foreign countries. I enjoyed the hospitality we received from our hotel staff and the vendors we came into contact with. I did, however, feel that we were cautiously spoon-fed information throughout the process. I felt we were manipulated as they showed us what they wanted us to see and told us what they wanted us to hear.

They took us to many historical places and gave us an unusual tale of communist half truths. They took us to visit an impoverished village, where I felt some staging had taken place. The biggest disappointment to me was all the unnecessary secrecy before, during, and after our journey. It felt kind of like a spy movie, not knowing what what was behind every door, especially the concealment of the orphanages to our group. As cooperative as our agency had been, they, too, refused to speak of visiting the orphanages. It had a feel of "don't rock the boat" to it.

I had no interest in disrupting their policies, but there were a few families that wanted to go and see the orphanages and were not allowed to do so. These are the things that really upset me about the process: all the unnecessary secrecy. I wanted to tell the story, not based on my disappointment with the program, but to let everyone who is waiting for their precious little one from China know that, although I struggled with the process, I was not disappointed with the results. I mentioned earlier that I learned much about myself during and after the adoption, and the one thing that stands out for me are the feelings I have for Samantha. I have never looked back at our decision to adopt, and when I hold Samantha, it's hard to imagine life before her. I am so deeply in love with this child. That being said, you can understand why I can reflect on all that Lorraine and I went through and when people ask, "Would you do it all again?" my answer is an unqualified "You betcha!"

CPSIA information can be obtained at www.ICGtesting.com
Printed in the USA
LVOW121820250912

300294LV00003B/47/P